"There are no two people that I have learned more from than Steve Stroope and Aubrey Malphurs. Steve is a brilliant pastor with incredible insights on information about churches. Aubrey's systems are always clear and accurate. I encourage every pastor and church planter to read this book from cover to cover."

—**Bob Roberts**, senior pastor, NorthWood Church; author, *Transformation* and *Glocalization*

"Few seminaries teach it, and fewer pastors find financial expertise in their nature or skill set. But strong financial management couldn't be more important to the success and health of a church. Aubrey Malphurs and Steven Stroope's *Money Matters in Church* fills a much needed gap of understanding for pastors and lay leaders. It is an excellent book for a church board's study together for the first thirty minutes of a year's board meetings. The smart pastor will share copies with his or her elders, board, and stewardship committee."

—**Ronald E. Keener**, editor, *Church Executive* magazine

"Some church leaders are hesitant to talk about money. But they shouldn't be. After all, Jesus talked about it more than he talked about prayer, heaven, or hell. And now Aubrey Malphurs and Steve Stroope have developed a 'how to' manual that not only gives the biblical support for teaching about money, but also reveals the step-by-step process of developing a community of givers and an attitude of gratitude in your church."

—**Ed Young**, senior pastor, Fellowship Church; author, *Outrageous, Contagious Joy*

"Money does matter! In this excellent book by Aubrey Malphers and Steve Stroope, you will be exposed to both the solid biblical principles and sound financial practices necessary for effective growth in a church of any size. With years of experience in both the academy and the development of a large church, they know what they are talking about. Don't miss out."

—**Bob Buford**, f   ership Network; authc   *Well*

"Money matters in the church because n all of us. Steve and Aubrey have provide combination of biblical teaching on money in the life of the church. This is must reading for any pa leader who wants to see the church maximize its financial resou for kingdom business."

—**Bryant Wright**, senior pastor, Johnson Ferry Baptist Church

"Great vision is only a pipe dream without resources. A principle job of a leader is securing resources for vision, and Steve Stroope and Aubrey Malphurs have provided a tool that is both biblically solid and intensely practical. The question we have been asking each other is, 'Where has this book been for our ministry up to now?'"

—**Jeff Jones**, senior pastor, Fellowship Bible Church North;
and **Gene A. Getz**, pastor emeritus, Fellowship Bible Church North;
director, Center for Church Renewal

"The Lord placed in my heart long ago that we are never more like Jesus than when we are giving. I have found that stewardship is one of the words that I would place in the top four of things that are most important in my life. I am grateful that Aubrey and Steven have brought their hearts and minds together to challenge us in managing resources that will one day change the world in which we live. This is a must-read!"

—**Johnny Hunt**, pastor, First Baptist Woodstock

"This fine work will provide pastors with a critical tool for understanding and addressing the financial needs of their churches. It's a practical book that will fill a void that has existed for too long in training of pastors for their fiscal management role in the church."

—**Tony Evans**, senior pastor, Oakcliff Bible Fellowship

Money Matters
in Church

Also by Aubrey Malphurs

Advanced Strategic Planning
Being Leaders
Biblical Manhood and Womanhood
Building Leaders (coauthor)
Church Next (coauthor)
A Contemporary Handbook for Weddings, Funerals,
*   and Other Occasions* (coauthor)
Developing a Dynamic Mission for Your Ministry
Developing a Vision for Ministry in the 21st Century
Doing Church
The Dynamics of Church Leadership
Leading Leaders
Maximizing Your Effectiveness
Ministry Nuts and Bolts
A New Kind of Church
Planting Growing Churches for the 21st Century
Pouring New Wine into Old Wineskins
Strategy 2000
Values-Driven Leadership
Vision America

Money Matters in Church

A Practical Guide for Leaders

Aubrey Malphurs and Steve Stroope

BakerBooks

Grand Rapids, Michigan

Published by Baker Books
a division of Baker Publishing Group
P.O. Box 6287, Grand Rapids, MI 49516-6287
www.bakerbooks.com

Printed in the United States of America

Library of Congress Cataloging-in-Publication Data
Malphurs, Aubrey.
    Money matters in church : a practical guide for leaders / Aubrey Malphurs and
Steve Stroope.
        p.   cm.
    Includes bibliographical references and index.
    ISBN 10: 0-8010-6627-1 (pbk.)
    ISBN 978-0-8010-6627-6 (pbk.)
    1. Church finance. I. Stroope, Steve, 1953– II. Title.
BV770.M35 2007
254'.8—dc22   2007006653

Laws relating to taxes, salaries, and contract labor may change from year to year. Though the authors have made every effort to present accurate and up-to-date information, the reader is responsible for knowing and abiding by current law.

Contents

Acknowledgments

Special thanks to Sandra Stanley, who did the hard work of making my thoughts legible, to the people of Lake Pointe and specifically the board of elders, who have allowed me the freedom to invest in the church beyond our local fellowship, and to Aubrey Malphurs, without whom I would not have been able to write my first book.

Steve Stroope

Thanks to my family for their support of my ministry—especially my wife, Susan. I also thank Sandra Stanley for all her hard work in making this book a reality.

Aubrey Malphurs

Introduction

Without question the area where most pastors feel least prepared to lead their churches is stewardship in general and church finances in particular. This is true regardless of the size of the church. Whether it is a congregation of fifteen people or fifteen thousand people, few leaders feel more than just adequate to lead in the financial aspects of their ministry. The problem, however, is that most churches expect and depend on their pastor not only to raise the finances but ensure that those finances are managed in a God-honoring way after they are collected. And if pastors don't know how or can't do it, then it won't get done, at least not well.

A number of you who picked up this book are seminary graduates with master's degrees, and some even have your doctorates. Here's the question: how many courses did you take in seminary on church finances? And for those of you who majored in pastoral ministries and leadership, how many of you took even a single course on church finances? At Dallas Theological Seminary where I (Aubrey) teach, I have a short unit on the pastor and finances. But this is rare for most seminaries. And when I introduce the topic, many of the students raise their eyebrows and get a pained expression on their faces. I know what they're thinking: *As a pastor, all I want to do is to teach and preach the Bible! I'm not good at arm-twisting and making people feel uncomfortable over money. And I don't want to add to the perception of those who think the church is only after their money. That's not who I am or what I want to do.*

This is where some pastors who come from the business world may have an advantage over the seminary graduate. Those who lead in the corporate world are expected to have a good knowledge of finances in order to run their company, or their particular branch of a large company, with integrity and competence. There are aspects of church finances, however, that are foreign even to those who have advanced degrees in business and finance.

The problem for the local church is that not only is it an organism (Paul compares it to the human body in 1 Corinthians 12:12–31), but it has a business aspect, with corporate responsibility to its constituents as well as the government.

The Importance of Church Finances

Why is the topic of church finances so important? The church's mission in this world, according to the Savior, is to make disciples (Matt. 28:19–20; Mark 16:15). As a part of discipleship, it is imperative that pastors hold their congregations accountable for their stewardship of God's resources in the same way that they would hold them accountable for any of the other biblical admonitions on discipleship.

One writer states that there are more than twenty-three hundred verses in the Bible that address the topic of money.[1] It's been noted that in Matthew 6:19–21 Jesus warns us against storing up temporal treasure on earth. Instead, he commands that we seek to store up eternal treasure in heaven. Then in verse 21, he explains why: "For where your treasure is, there your heart will be also." How can we know where our hearts are? By looking for our treasure. And one key to discovering our treasure is what we do with our money. Sometimes people fool us. If we listen to them and watch what they do when they're around us at church, they appear to have it all together. They seem to be spiritual giants. However, one of the true tests of where they are spiritually is to examine their checkbooks.

Congregational giving is about much more than simply giving money to the church. It's a faith issue. It addresses matters of the heart. And a person cannot become a mature believer if his or her financial house is not in order. A leader's responsibility is to set a good example by protecting and managing properly the resources entrusted to him.

How the Church Is Doing

If what we do with our money is a strong indicator of our spiritual maturity, then we must ask, How are we doing? And early in the twenty-first century, we must ask, How is the church of Jesus Christ doing when it comes to investing its money in kingdom work?

Barna Research reports that in 2004 nearly four out of every five adults gave money to one or more nonprofit organizations. Of these nonprofit organizations, the church received the largest share (two-thirds or 65 percent of all adults donated money to a church in 2004).[2] The average amount of money that Americans gave to churches was $895 per donor per year (which is approximately $75 a month). While this is more than the average amounts they've given in the past, when one factors in inflation, this figure proves to be about 2 percent less than what the church received in 1999.[3]

When addressing church finances, many pastors and their people speak of tithing—the practice of giving at least 10 percent of one's income to a church and/or parachurch ministry. Barna reports: "Only 4 percent gave such an amount to churches alone; just 6 percent gave to either churches or to a combination of churches and parachurch ministries."[4] Therefore the answer to our question—How is the church doing in investing in Christ's kingdom?—is that it's not doing well at all.

Why People Don't Give More

These numbers raise another question: why don't people give more money? When Barna Research addressed this issue, they found five significant barriers to more generous giving.

> Some people lack the motivation to give away their hard-earned money because the church has failed to provide a compelling vision for how the money will make a difference in the world. These are donors who can find other uses for their money and are not excited about simply handing money over to the church. The second group is those who see their giving as leverage on the future. They withhold money from the church because they do not see a sufficient return on their investment. The third segment is comprised of people who do not realize the church needs their money to be effective. Their church has done an inadequate job of asking for money, so people remain oblivious to the church's expectations and potential. The fourth group is composed of those who are ignorant of what the Bible teaches about our responsibility to apply God's resources in ways that affect lives. The final category contains those who are just selfish. They figure they worked hard for their money and it's theirs to use as they please. Their priorities revolve around their personal needs and desires.[5]

While the Barna research paints a dismal picture of the church's finances in general, we believe that none of these reasons or any others that we've heard are insurmountable. Actually, we view the future with much hope for the church. We are convinced that these are leadership issues that can be addressed and overcome. And that is our plan for this book. Barna concludes: "The reality is that Americans are willing to give more generously than they typically do, but it takes a purposeful and well-executed approach to facilitate that generosity."[6] That is the purpose of this book—to provide you as leaders with a purposeful and well-executed approach to win back the hearts and the pocketbooks of your people, and then to manage the finances of your church in a way that will maximize your effectiveness. We can do much better and, for the sake of Christianity in America and beyond, we must do better.

Is This Book for You?

We believe that the church is the hope of the world and that Spirit-filled leaders are the hope of the church. Therefore we've written this book primarily for those who lead churches: pastors, executive and administrative pastors, church staff, finance committees, lay leaders, governing boards, consultants, and any others who deal in any way with finances. If you really want to know and lead the church in the area of church finances, this is the book for you. We suspect that parachurch ministries would benefit from these principles as well. In addition, seminaries would be wise to incorporate the book's contents into any classes for pastoral preparation.

I (Aubrey) have pastored three churches (one was a church plant and the other two were revitalization ministries). I have also been on the faculty of Dallas Seminary for twenty-six years and have served as a church consultant for the last ten to fifteen years. Thus I approach the topic of stewardship and finances as a pastor, seminary professor, and church consultant who has worked with churches of various sizes.

I (Steve) am currently serving Lake Pointe Church in Rockwall, Texas, where I have been the pastor for over twenty-five years. (I'm Aubrey's pastor.) Lake Pointe is a multisite church that sees an average of ten thousand attendees every weekend. Yes, it's a megachurch, and that could prove to be a turnoff for you, especially if you lead or are a part of a smaller church. However, you must realize that I became Lake Pointe's pastor in 1980 when its average attendance was fifty-seven. The point is that I have pastored the church at its various sizes, from fifty-seven to ten thousand–plus attendees, so I've been where most of you are. We've tried to be sensitive to various contexts in writing this book.

Where We're Going

If you take a quick glance at the contents, you'll see that we've divided *Money Matters in Church* into three sections that will give you an idea of the journey ahead. Part 1 addresses creating a culture of giving. Part 2 deals with managing your kingdom resources, and part 3 goes into detail about planning for and carrying out a capital campaign.

If you're a senior pastor, the point person of a parachurch ministry, or a consultant, you should first work through this material on your own. When you feel that you've grasped its contents, you would be wise to go through the material again with your staff and key leaders.

If you're a church planter, you have the easier job. You don't have to address any financial sacred cows that have been in place for years other than any that a denomination may impose on you. Read this book and apply the various principles as the church grows and develops under your leadership.

If you're a seminary professor, you could assign this book as must-reading for your students, or you could assign it as a course project. Divide the class into teams and ask them to find a church in the area that would serve as a real-life lab for a project where the students would apply the principles of this book to that church and its finances.

All readers would be wise to answer the questions at the end of the chapters. We have designed them to help you think through and apply the contents of the chapter to your unique ministry situation.

Part 1

Creating a Culture of Giving

It's imperative that every pastor know what the Bible says about finances before trying to talk to his people about them. Chapter 1 presents a biblical theology of stewardship, focusing on finances, and serves as the foundation for the rest of the book. Chapter 2 will help you learn how to develop your donors, while chapter 3 will teach you how to maximize contributions.

$\gtrless1\lessgtr$

Developing and Communicating Your Theology of Financial Stewardship

The focus of this chapter and the basis for this book is financial stewardship in relation to the church. Pastors must know and be able to communicate to their congregation a theology of financial stewardship. We address this in the very first chapter because a theology of financial stewardship is the foundation on which the rest of this book will build. We can't emphasize enough the importance of the leader's knowledge of what Scripture teaches about this important topic.

The aim of this chapter is to help you think about and, if you have not already done so, develop your own theology of financial stewardship. Based on what Scripture says about financial stewardship in general and what God expects from the church and its leaders in particular, we will walk you through the necessary steps that will help you develop your theology of financial stewardship. You can read ours in appendix A, but we ask that you not consult it until after you've developed your own.

At the end of this chapter we will address briefly the communication of your theology of financial stewardship. Developing and knowing what the Bible teaches on this topic isn't enough. Church leaders must communicate that knowledge to their people, so all can apply its truth to their lives.

The following is an overview of the process you might follow in developing your theology. To begin with, you'll need to look at the concept of biblical stewardship in the Old Testament, for that is the foundation for and context in which to best understand financial stewardship. Then study financial stewardship in the New Testament, focusing on the local church.

Stewardship in the Old Testament

Biblical Stewardship

The Old Testament teaches about what belongs to God. We suggest you consider the following key passages: 1 Chronicles 29:11, 16; Psalm 24:1–2; 50:10–12; 89:11. Think about what God has done with what belongs to him, as seen in the role he assigned to Adam in Genesis 1:28 and 2:15. Did the fall have any impact on this?

Financial Stewardship

With this initial understanding of biblical stewardship in place, you're ready to explore what the Old Testament says about financial steward-ship. We'll begin with money in general, explore material blessing, and then the concept of tithing. Much of what the Old Testament teaches about money is found in the wisdom literature. What do Proverbs 17:16 and Ecclesiastes 5:10 tell you about money?

What does the Old Testament generally teach about how God re-sponds to those who honor him with their possessions (see Prov. 3:9–10; 11:24–25)? You'll find an example of God's blessing in Genesis 14:18–20. Also Proverbs 28:27; Psalm 37:22; and 112:1–3 will provide you with additional insight.

When it comes to tithing, we must warn you that there is a wide range of opinions on what the Old Testament teaches about tithing, so don't be too hard on yourself if you struggle a little with this information.

To determine what the Old Testament says about tithing, first look at what it teaches about tithing before Moses gave the law to Israel at Sinai. Two key passages are Genesis 14:20 and 28:22. Some use these two texts to teach that God's people tithed before the Mosaic law was given. Therefore tithing isn't limited only to those under the law and is for today. Do you agree?

Under the law there may have been several mandatory tithes, but the actual number is debatable. Be aware of this as you work through the following texts that address the number of tithes: Leviticus 27:30–32; Numbers 18:21–24, 27; Deuteronomy 12:4–19; 14:22–23, 28–29; 26:12–13; and Nehemiah 10:34–39. What is your conclusion about the number of tithes that Israel gave?

You would be wise at this point to ponder how tithing related to worship under the law. Also Malachi 3:8–10 addresses the gravity of not tithing to God, so be sure to look it up.

God instructed Israel to bring their tithes to a certain place (see Deut. 12:5–7, 12, 17–18). We read in Exodus 33:7–11 where this place was initially. Later it was the temple. Malachi 3:10 tells specifically where in the temple the tithes were brought. Read 1 Kings 7:51; Nehemiah 10:38; and 13:12 to see what else was kept there. For additional insight, read Acts 4:34–35 to see where the early church brought its money.

Later in Israel's history the practice of tithing was expanded. Did all Israelites tithe initially? Surprisingly the answer is no. The Torah didn't impose any tithe on people in some occupations, such as fishing or trading. We see in Matthew 23:23 and Luke 11:42 that the Pharisees pushed tithing to an extreme. Many of the church fathers supported tithing of all incomes, not just agricultural products.

Stewardship in the New Testament

Biblical Stewardship

The New Testament picks up on the biblical stewardship theme of the Old Testament and develops it further. This can provide a context for your teachings on financial stewardship. You'll need to examine both.

The New Testament Greek word for steward is *oikonomos*. In the NIV translation of Luke 12:42, it is translated "manager." In the classical Greek the manager or *oikonomos* handled the business affairs of a household.

Jesus provides his primary teaching on stewardship in his parables found in the Gospels. He uses *oikonomos* (manager) twice—once in the parable of the servants (Luke 12:42–48) and again in the parable of the shrewd manager (16:1–13)—to illustrate stewardship truths. In Luke 12:42–48 Jesus uses the stewardship metaphor to call his disicples to be faithful followers; unfaithfulness would prove costly. In Luke 16:1–13 Jesus teaches that God has entrusted us as his stewards with that which is temporary (worldly wealth) to provide for that which is eternal (true riches).

Jesus's concept of stewardship is foundational to many of the other parables, as we indicated in the introduction to this book. You would profit much by reading these parables and jotting down any lessons or principles about stewardship you find in them.

Financial Stewardship

With this further understanding of biblical stewardship, you're ready to turn to the New Testament direct teaching on financial stewardship. You'll need to look at Jesus's teaching on finances, the early churches and finances, Paul's teaching on giving, and other writers' teachings on finances.

Jesus's Key Teachings on Finances

The following treatment is not meant to be exhaustive but representative of Jesus's teachings on finances found primarily in the Gospels. These are most instructive for Jesus's disciples in today's churches regarding their giving. As you develop your theology of financial stewardship, consider the following questions (note that many of the answers are found in appendix A):

1. What principle does Jesus teach in Luke 16:10–15 about the two masters—God and money?
2. What does Jesus teach us about how to give in Matthew 6:1–4? How important are one's motives to what one gives?
3. According to Matthew 6:19–24, the Savior teaches us where we should store up our money. What does this reveal about where our hearts are and what we truly value in life?
4. What does Jesus teach about the material needs of his true disciples in Matthew 6:25–34?
5. What does the Lord teach us about how much we should give in Mark 12:41–43? Who gave more: the widow or the rich man?
6. According to Acts 20:35, which is more important: giving or receiving? This is a passage where Paul quotes Jesus, but the quote is not found in the Gospels. Of course it is still instructive. What do you learn from this?
7. What does the Savior's experience in Luke 8:1–3 teach about workers in the church receiving financial support? Some argue that receiving such support is wrong. What do you think?

The Early Churches and Finances

The book of Acts provides us with a limited picture of how early, young churches handled their finances. We'll look at two of them. The first is the church at Jerusalem (Acts 2 and 4–5), and the second is the church at Antioch (Acts 11). Several other passages, such as 1 Corinthians 9 and 1 Timothy 5, also address financial aspects of the New Testament church.

As you examine these passages, be careful to distinguish between descriptive and prescriptive passages. Descriptive passages tell us what took place but don't require anything of the reader. Prescriptive passages tell us that there is something we must do. Also do not assume that all churches handled their finances in the same way. Just because one church held a certain practice doesn't mean that all other churches did the same.

The first primary text is Acts 2:42–47. In what is a progress report, Luke provides in verses 31–41 a brief summary of how the Jerusalem church was doing. Then he gives us a glimpse of how the church used its finances. We see in verses 44–45 how the early church took care of its needy people.

In verse 44 Luke tells us all the believers had "everything in common." Verse 45 clarifies further what this meant. The believers were willing to sell what they owned to provide for those with legitimate needs. Acts 5:1–4 may add to your understanding of this.

In Acts 4:32–5:4 Luke emphasizes how the young church was unified, as manifested by people's willingness to share their personal possessions and to sell land and houses to meet the needs of others. However, a problem surfaces. In the story of Ananias, Luke teaches us about the importance of motives in our giving. In this account Luke also gives us some insight as to who in the church handled the money from the sales and how they handled that money (see 4:34–37 and 5:2). Acts 6:1–6 will add to your understanding of the responsibilities of leaders in regard to the church's money.

We find one further reference to the church and finances in Acts 11:27–30. In verses 27–28 Luke presents a problem that the new church in Antioch addressed—a severe famine that would affect the Jerusalem church. This would be similar to the natural disasters that we see today, such as those caused by earthquakes, hurricanes, and so forth. The believers at Antioch decided that they would provide help for the believers living in Judea. Here we discover five practices. The following questions will help you discover these practices:

1. From whom did the church seek funding? Was it from individuals within the church or some established fund of the church?
2. How much did each person give (v. 29)?
3. To whom did they give this money? Was it to believers or unbelievers or both? What does this teach, if anything, about how churches should respond to natural disasters that affect unbelievers today?
4. To whom did they send their gifts and why? What might Acts 4:34–37 and 5:2 add to the answer?
5. Finally, who actually took the gift to Antioch? What does this teach about how we should handle funds? Compare to 2 Corinthians 8:18–21.

What does this section on the early church and its finances say about the church's remuneration of those involved in its ministry? Is it okay for churches to pay some of those who serve in its ministry, such as its pastors? Acts doesn't comment on clergy remuneration, but Paul does in 1 Corinthians 9 and 1 Timothy 5:17–18. What do these passages teach?

Paul's Teaching on Giving

In Romans 12:8 and 2 Corinthians 8–9, Paul gives instruction on biblical giving. In Romans 12:8 he teaches about the spiritual gift of giving. See Ephesians 4:28 for additional insight.

In 2 Corinthians 8–9 Paul addresses three key areas of New Testament giving in the context of the church: how to give, how much to give, and the benefits of giving. First, read these two chapters and make a list of what Paul teaches about how to give. For example, in 8:3 and 5 he says that Christians are to give as much as we are able. There are twelve teachings here on how to give.

Next, list what Paul teaches on how much to give. What does God expect us to give? What or how much is good giving? For example, in 8:2–3; 9:5–6, 11 he teaches that we should give generously. We found four teachings on how much to give.

Finally, examine 9:6–15 for Paul's teaching on the benefits of giving. Here Paul explains that there are at least three benefits to good giving.

What about the tithe? What does the New Testament teach about tithing? Does it prescribe or mandate that good Christian givers tithe? Tithing is mentioned in Matthew 23:23; Luke 18:12; and Hebrews 7:1–10. Some Christians teach that tithing was mandated and practiced under Mosaic law, and since believers are not under law (Rom. 10:4; Eph. 2:14–16; Heb. 8:13) but grace (Gal. 3:1–25), we aren't obligated to tithe. Do you agree or disagree? If you believe that Christians today should tithe, then how much must one tithe? Under the Mosaic law there were several mandatory tithes.

Other Teaching on Giving

In their writings James and John address aspects of giving that affect the local church. James brings up finances in James 2:1–13. Look for the message and the warning that are there. In 3 John the author addresses the issue of whether believers should solicit funds from unbelievers. What is his conclusion?

Communicating Your Theology of Financial Stewardship

After you have developed your theology of financial stewardship, it will serve as a rich reservoir for communicating vital financial truth to your people.

When we refer to *communicating* the theology, we are referring primarily to the church's preaching and teaching ministry. The pastor is responsible to see that this communication takes place. However, this teaching must not end with him. The pastor is also responsible to see that others in the ministry communicate these truths as well. This would include those on the pastoral staff, any governing board, and the church's lay leadership, especially its teachers.

This assumes that all are in basic agreement with the pastor's theology of finances. It's futile to expect that all will agree on every point, but it is important that all agree on what is prescriptive and clearly mandated by the Bible, such as the remuneration of pastors, generous giving, and so on. Since the pastor is the primary leader of the church and its key teacher, we believe that other leaders should defer to him and his direction for the church.

There are two basic ways to communicate your theology of finances. The first is informally. In informal conversation you can tell others what you believe. This is an effective way of communicating truth and may make more of an impresion than the same message given in a more formal spoken or written format.

There are times, however, when formal communication is necessary. Formal settings in which you can communicate to the church the theology of financial stewardship include sermons, Sunday school or adult Bible fellowships (ABFs), small groups, new members classes, counseling sessions, workshops, seminars, town hall meetings, letters from the pastor, and church newsletters. We will elaborate on some of these in the next chapter.

Questions for Reflection, Discussion, and Application

1. Do you agree with the authors' stress on developing a theology of financial stewardship before you pursue the topic of church stewardship and finances? Why or why not?
2. Did you take the time to work through the questions and develop an initial theology of stewardship and finances? If you didn't, why not? Will you do this sometime soon, preferably before you go any farther in this book? If not, then when will you do this?
3. Did you read over the authors' theology of financial stewardship in appendix A? If so, how did your theology of finances compare to theirs? On what aspects did you disagree and why?
4. Do you agree that it's important for you to communicate your theology of financial stewardship to your church? Why or why

not? If you communicate your theology of financial stewardship, when and how often do you do it?

5. As you read through the authors' suggestions for communicating formally your theology of financial stewardship, what are some vehicles that would work in your ministry? Which have you already used? Which new ones could you use?

⨂2⨂

Developing Donors

In the introduction to this book, we said that the responsibility for raising funds in a church falls squarely in the lap of the senior pastor. Whether we like it or not, that's how most church cultures operate. Bill Hybels compares financial sources to a river and correctly observes: "And like it or not, it is the leader's job to create that river and to manage it wisely. The sooner the leader realizes that the better."[1]

In chapter 1 we helped you think through a biblical theology of financial stewardship. In this chapter we'll consider how pastors raise the needed finances: the simple answer is that they must develop donors. We suggest six means that pastors could use to develop their donors and raise the ministry's operational funds.

Regularly Cast the Church's Vision

First, you must regularly cast a clear, compelling vision for the church. The key to cultivating donors for your church's ministry is vision. Our experience is that people are not that interested in just paying the light bills or staff salaries, nor do they respond well to guilt trips, negativism, or shortages. People give to big, dynamic visions that, in turn, produce the passion that is vital to giving. They are more willing to invest in "what could be" (future possibilities) than "what is" (present reality), especially if "what is" is floundering or in the red. The exception is when "what is" is obviously blessed of God and growing spiritually and numerically.

To a certain degree, raising finances is a vision measure. What does that mean? People's giving response will often tell you something about the quality of your church's vision and the leader's ability to cast that vision. The people can know what the church's vision is only through the vision caster and how that person articulates and frames it. Thus a pastor who fails to or cannot effectively cast the vision will have a negative impact on the church's income. In chapter 13 we'll say more about vision and how to communicate one. You must communicate it well and cast it over and over in every way possible.

Implement a Churchwide Stewardship Education Plan

One of the most effective ways of developing donors is to implement a churchwide stewardship education plan. This involves developing and implementing a strategy for building biblical training into your ministry. Scripture has much to say about giving, and this forms the basis for your stewardship plan. Effective communication vehicles will assist your people in becoming mature givers. We strongly encourage you to utilize all of the following seven communication vehicles, which will work together in your church to enhance stewardship education.

Sermons

As we said in chapter 1, the first and most important step that a pastor or leader can take in developing donors is discovering what the Bible says about stewardship and then teaching these truths consistently to his or her people. Leaders should not wait until there's a dire financial need in the church to address the issue of stewardship. Somebody once said that God is not in the business of raising money; he's in the business of raising Christians. The issue of stewardship is more about the development of the believer than it is about the financial condition of the local church. As we grow our people and teach them what the Bible says about stewardship, they mature and learn to give. Every time they give, they learn to give away a little of their selfishness.

Some leaders shirk this responsibility. They may fear what their people or "seekers" might think. Many pastors want to please their people and be liked, which is normal; however, a significant difference exists between being liked and being respected. Jesus did not hesitate to address people in the area of their finances (see Matt. 6:19–24), and pastors must not either. Many people really do want to know what the Bible teaches about money because it is an issue that is so close to their heart. They realize that their finances are not providing true happiness and they want to know the truth. People of God must know the Word of God, and pastors must be truth tellers.

When Paul left the church at Ephesus, he declared that he was free from the blood of all men because he had not shied away from sharing "the whole will of God" (Acts 20:26–27). Part of that full counsel is what the Bible says about stewardship. Pastors and Christian leaders must not avoid the topic because they feel uncomfortable speaking about it. If God's messenger is true to the Word, he must teach about giving. There is more written in the New Testament concerning giving than about heaven and hell combined. It's a message that is appropriate whether the church is in financial need or not, and if it's consistently taught, the church should not get into a financial crisis.

The Malphurs Group gives the churches that it works with an online Church Giving Inventory that asks the congregation key questions, such as whether they believe the pastor preaches too much on money or not enough. It also asks if they feel that they know what the Bible teaches about finances along with a number of other issues. We have found that most congregations believe the pastor does not preach enough on the topic, and they want to know more. This comes as a surprise to most pastors.

How often should pastors preach and teach on stewardship and biblical giving? Some pastors set aside one month each year for positive, motivating biblical instruction on giving. George Barna notes that pastors who preach two or more messages in a series usually receive a better response than those who preach on the topic only once a year or in several messages spread out over the year.[2] We suggest that you approach your messages along the lines that giving is a privilege as much as it is a responsibility. Resist the temptation to bang your people over the head with biblical imperatives. Instead, assume that they want to give and you are there to help them enjoy the privilege of giving to God.

The pastor should expand his preaching on money beyond just giving. Sermon series could also address such topics as debt, saving, and our attitude toward money. Messages on stewardship should include encouragement concerning contributions of time and talents and the stewardship of influence.

Sunday School

Sunday school is another excellent place to train your people in giving. Take three or four sessions annually to cover some aspect of stewardship in your Sunday school or small-group ministry. An example could be a series titled "Managing Your Money God's Way." The lessons could be coordinated with the pastor's sermons, either preceding them or following up on the theme. The same biblical text, or a different one that expands on the theme, could be used. When a Sunday school lesson follows a sermon on the same finances or giving theme, there is time to discuss the meaning of the message and ways to apply it. Another option is to cover the topic of finances in Sunday school but not at the same time as the sermon series. The advantage here is that you would cover biblical stewardship during more weeks of the year.

Small Groups

Small groups in a church can also make a big difference and play a significant role in donor development. One of the reasons some churches struggle financially is that they have a weak or nonexistent small-group ministry. We believe there are three key structures in the church that can be used for disciple making: the large gathering (worship), the midsize group (Sunday school or Bible fellowships), and small groups. Each has its unique benefits. Stewardship can be taught in the large gathering, but financial accountability and encouragement take place in the midsize or small group. Small-group leaders need to catch a vision of disciple making and be responsible for seeing that everyone in their group finds a place of service, is reading the Word of God, participates in evangelism, and is a fully participating partner in terms of stewardship.

Small-group leaders should not have access to the church's financial records and should not confront people on their specific financial giving. However, it is in the small group that stewardship is modeled, giving experiences are shared, and one-on-one encouragement is exercised to facilitate good stewardship. The small-group leader can share with the group the need for everyone to participate financially in the church and give testimony of his or her own participation (without, of course, sharing inappropriate details).

We recommend that stewardship lessons be scheduled from time to time in the small or midsize group. This gives the leader a vehicle to discuss these issues. As we suggested earlier, these lessons could follow up the sermon with discussion and application. Another good option for small groups is a more in-depth, twelve-week study on finances, using material from an organization such as Crown Financial Ministries (www.crown.org).

New Members Class

When people decide to become members, they are very interested in and committed to the church and its ministry. For this reason it puzzles us that some churches don't have a membership class or workshop. Wise churches provide a new members class or workshop to orient them to the church and its expectations. It is critical that they cover matters such as the church's values, mission, vision, and strategy for alignment purposes. However, this is also a great time for the church to clearly communicate its giving expectations and the biblical basis for them. In the Lake Pointe congregation, we conduct a new members workshop that every adult believer is required to attend before his or her membership process is complete.

Famed Oklahoma football coach Bud Wilkinson once described a football game as twenty-two people in desperate need of rest being watched by thousands of people in desperate need of exercise. Unfortunately in some churches there are a few people who do the giving and the rest just watch. During Lake Pointe's workshop, we let all our new members know they are no longer spectators. They are now not only a part of the family but also a part of the team, and we expect them to participate in the strategy and the goals, and the purpose that God has given to us as a church.

We ask our members to commit themselves to do the following: get involved in a small group; find a place to serve; seek to befriend those who are lost, pray for them, witness to them, and invite them to Lake Pointe; and support the church financially in a God-honoring way.

During the workshop, we teach that we believe biblical giving is systematic, proportional, and sacrificial. It's systematic in that we want our church members to decide how often they're going to give and then to give, without the church always having to plead for it. In the same way that they pay their mortgage and their car loan on a regular basis, they should give faithfully and regularly to the church. In other words, biblical giving is consistent giving. If people are paid once a month, we suggest that they give once a month; if they are paid weekly, they could give weekly, as the Lord blesses them. The important point isn't so much when to give but that giving should be a regular habit. That way, we don't have to waste precious time in a worship service pleading for funds that our church members should be giving on a regular basis without being asked.

Also biblical giving is proportional. Proportional giving teaches that if God has blessed you with much financially, then you should give much financially. If he's just blessed you a little financially, then you should just give a little. And if God has not blessed you financially at all, then you're off the hook.

Finally, we teach that biblical giving is sacrificial. It should change your lifestyle. If we give a convenient gift that can be given without much thought—without any prayer—if we can reach into our wallet or purse or write a check and it doesn't really change anything in terms of our values or our lifestyle, then it doesn't meet the criteria of being sacrificial. At our new member workshop we do not ask the member to write down a specific percentage or a particular amount he or she is going to give, but to make a written commitment that as long as they are a member of Lake Pointe, that he or she will give to God, through the local church, in a God-honoring way.

Some visitors from other churches who have heard about our workshop commitment have asked, "Do you throw people out of your church if they don't keep the commitment they made?" We thought long and hard about that before we made a decision that we would not confront people personally if they were not faithful in their giving. However, we do address it on a corporate level. From time to time, I (Steve) will address the church and talk about the percentage of our people who gave absolutely nothing to the church in the previous twelve months and the percentage of people who are obviously giving less than they should be giving in relation to their income. Also I comment on the percentage of our people who give less than eighteen hundred dollars a year (which would be less than a tithe of a poverty-level income for a family of three). Finally, in a public worship service, several times a year, I remind our people of the fivefold commitment they made and that keeping our commitment helps the church fulfill our vision.

One other thing we do at Lake Pointe in our new members workshop is to give every new member of our church *The Treasure Principle* by Randy Alcorn.[3] I'm sure there are other publications that can give a good theological presentation of the church's position on stewardship. The great thing about this particular book is that it's about a forty-five-minute read. It's a good summary of biblical stewardship. So when you provide somebody with such a book or theology on stewardship that's an easy read, you empower them by giving them that knowledge.

Counseling

Along with the various ministries that teach on biblical giving, we believe the church needs to provide some counseling for those who are struggling with debt and other similar financial problems. Because we are a large church, we have been able to set up our own Financial Fitness Counseling Center that helps our people address any debt, establish personal budgets, and pursue financial planning. It is similar to a consumer credit counseling center. We provide fee-based counseling, although scholarships are available. A smaller church may not be able to provide the same in-house service but could refer members to agencies in their community that offer such services or join with other churches to set up such a center.

Information on Deferred Giving

Early in the twenty-first century in America, there are more affluent people than ever before, and many of them are members of our churches. While most have estate plans, they have not included the church in them. We argue that the church has a responsibility to inform people of the opportunity to have a lasting impact on the church through estate giving. I (Aubrey) address this in more detail in my book *Advanced Strategic Planning*.[4]

Workshops and Seminars

The church should consider offering quarterly or semiannual workshops on a variety of financial aspects, such as budgeting, investing, estate planning, retirement, and other similar topics of interest. Consider inviting unchurched people from the community to the workshops, providing them with a positive, practical exposure to the church. At Lake Pointe we share what the Bible has to say about finances in a six-week seminar titled "Extreme Stewardship." This series is taught by a financial advisor and consists of six one-and-one-half-hour modules that cover the following topics: biblical foundation, debt, investing, giving, estate planning, and cultural stewardship. We charge thirty dollars per individual and fifty dollars per couple to cover the cost of materials. (We've discovered that when people pay for a class and its materials, they take it more seriously and value it more.)

A Churchwide Stewardship Education Plan

Sermons

Sunday school/adult Bible Fellowships

Small groups

New members classes

Counseling

Information on deferred giving

Workshops and seminars

Constantly Communicate with the Congregation

When consulting with churches, we like to stress how important it is that the leadership communicate regularly with the congregation. This is a third way to develop donors. Someone has said, "If people don't trust you, you cannot lead them." The same holds true for raising finances. If the people do not trust you, they will not give! Why would they contribute funds to those whom they do not trust? A lack of trust develops when leadership keeps people in the dark, for whatever reason. Rick Warren says that "people are down on what they're not up on." Thus, if you are having problems in this area, ask yourself, *Does the congregation trust the leadership?*

Constant communication and transparency create a sense of ownership that inevitably invites people to become donors and support the ministry. You tend to support that which is yours. Barna writes: "Remember: people cannot own a ministry they do not understand, and people cannot understand it if they are not kept up to date about its status."[5]

How can you practice constant communication? We discussed this in chapter 1. There must be both informal and formal communication. Encourage the strategic leadership team or any others who might be spearheading a campaign or the regular weekly administrators of funds to share informally with people what is going on.

To communicate formally, you can have one-way communication through bulletins, newsletters, personal letters, video announcements, and public testimonies from individual givers. Two-way communication could be done through online chat rooms, town hall meetings, personal telephone calls, and listening groups.

When communicating with your people, be sure to use lots of personal stories about how people's lives are being changed through the ministry of the church. This helps your people see that finances are really about people and about expanding the mission of the church. In any of these formats, you would typically say less about numbers, but more about the ministry that the money provides. When people see changed lives, money is going to flow toward those kinds of results and that kind of vision.

A method that does not work well is inserting notices in the church bulletin or newsletter that say that the church is short on money or that the offerings are far behind in terms of the annual budget. If you're going to express a need to your people, it must be personal and specific. For example, show some pictures of some kids and announce, "We need to build a new wing for our children," or talk about the concerns of young people and the need to start a new program to reach them.

Saying, "We have a general budget, and we're thirty-two thousand dollars behind" doesn't inspire people. In fact it makes people think, *Well, maybe we have too big of a budget,* or *Maybe the money's not being managed well.* People don't give to a dying ministry; they give to vision. They give to the future. They give to help people, reach people, or develop people for God's glory.

Challenge People to Make an Annual Commitment

Another way to develop donors is to challenge them annually to commit or recommit to giving. At Lake Pointe we ask for this commitment in the large-group settings. We ask our people to recommit to the five areas of involvement that we first introduce in the new members workshop. Most years we will make this very specific by asking them to write their commitments on a commitment card (see sample on next page). For example, we may ask them to commit to a small group and give the name of that small group. We ask them to list the ministries where they're currently serving in the church or to indicate where they would be willing to serve. We ask them to write down the names of those they're praying for and seeking to invite to Lake Pointe. We encourage them to share the specifics on their financial commitment—to pledge a specific amount that they will give to missions, to the building fund, and to the general fund in the coming year. Other years we ask for the same commitments without the specifics. Asking for the commitments in a variety of ways keeps the process from becoming routine.

Other years we don't press for all the details but ask the people to make a general commitment to the same five areas. We understand that some church cultures respond better to more of a soft-sell approach. If this is true of your church, ask for the general commitment without requesting specific details of how much people are going to give to a specific fund. Some churches have chosen to make the commitment card with two parts. One part indicates a general commitment, and this is the part the member turns in to the church. The other part provides for more specific information to be entered. The member keeps this part for his or her own records.

As the circumstances in people's lives change, an opportunity to pledge annually helps people renew their commitment to serve, witness, and give financially. Most of your people get a raise every year. The annual commitment allows them once a year to sit down and, even if they don't tell you the amount of their gift, reexamine how God has blessed them and then decide how to respond in a proportionate way.

Conduct Capital Campaigns

We strongly encourage churches to conduct capital campaigns on a regular basis to fund special projects, such as missions, the purchase of property, new construction, facility relocation or renovation, debt reduction, and other key projects that require monies over and above the general fund. Though missions should already be included in the

Dear People of Lake Pointe,

Every year we invite our members and regular attenders to recommit themselves to five basic Christian disciplines that reflect the values that are expressed in what we call the Five Ws. We believe fully-developing followers of Christ are committed to:

Worshipping God
Contributing to God's **W**ork
Living under the authority of God's **W**ord
Walking with God's people, and
Impacting God's **W**orld

You are invited, as a member of Lake Pointe, to utilize the enclosed commitment card in indicating your desire to fully participate in the ministry of Lake Pointe Church in 2007. The five values listed inside represent what I believe to be reasonable commitments for those who have a true desire to see the Lake Pointe dream become reality. Please pray about these vital areas.

Bring this form with you the weekend of January 20/21. Don't worry if you are unable at this time to provide all the specifics asked for on the form. That is why a duplicate card has been provided for you to keep. Give as much information as possible on the church's copy when you make your commitment and then fill in the details on your own copy as you discover the particulars throughout the year.

It is a privilege to be a partner with you in this vital endeavor. Thank you for making a difference in the lives of so many.

Steve Stroope

Pastor Steve

My Commitment (Church's Copy)

☐ LAKE POINTE MEMBER ☐ REGULAR ATTENDER BUT NOT YET A MEMBER
                                          ☐ Would like to join now

Name (His): _____ _____ Birthdate

Name (Hers): _____ _____ Birthdate

Home Phone Number: _____

Address: _____

City: _____ State: _____ Zip: _____

Email: ☐☐☐☐☐☐☐☐☐☐☐☐☐☐☐☐☐☐☐☐☐☐☐☐☐☐☐☐

Campus I/we attend: ☐ Rockwall ☐ Town East ☐ Sulphur Springs ☐ Firewheel

In response to God's love for me and my desire to share His love with others, I commit to the following in 2007 *(Married couples, please respond individually in the spaces provided,)*:

☐ **To be involved in study, fellowship, and care in a Bible Fellowship:**
   My Bible Fellowship (if known): _____
   ☐ I/we would like some help in finding a Bible Fellowship.

☐ **To establish a regular time of personal prayer and Bible study:**
   My Daily Time Alone With God: AM/PM   AM/PM
                                          HIS   *HERS*

☐ **To use my abilities to serve in a ministry:**
   For help in finding a ministry, visit the Volunteer Center.

☐ **To pray for, witness to, and invite others to come hear about God's love:**

   Unchurched I'm   1. _____ / _____
   praying for and   *HIS*   *HERS*
   seeking to invite: 2. _____ / _____
                                   HIS   *HERS*
                           3. _____ / _____
                                   HIS   *HERS*

☐ **To financially support the ministries of Lake Pointe in a God-honoring manner:**
   My Estimated Gifts In 2007:
   • General Fund _____ • Mission Fund _____ • Building Fund _____
                             (including Compassion gifts)

Please return during the worship service the weekend of January 20/21.

budget, a capital campaign is an effective tool to raise additional funds for expanding your mission's network as well.

Most churches can conduct an effective capital campaign every three years, although many churches will hold fewer than this. Generally the campaign goal should be in the range of one to two times the average annual budget, and some campaigns will raise more. The campaign itself usually lasts six to ten weeks, culminating in a commitment service when people may give a one-time offering as well as pledge to give to the campaign over and above their normal giving—a sacrificial gift. The pledges will come in over the next one to three years. The pledge approach helps churches plan when and how they will use funds.

The best time to conclude a campaign is December, because the person's one-time gift and three years of pledges will cover four tax periods. We like these campaigns because they serve to provide a necessary "kick in the pants" to promote sacrificial giving and raise money that would not be given to the general fund. Many churches report that their general giving actually increases during a campaign and remains higher afterward.

A number of churches are using consultants to help them conduct their capital campaigns. If you have never led a capital campaign, it is a good idea to use outside help. There are aspects to a successful campaign that consultants have tested and refined through their involvement in multiple campaigns, and their experience will maximize the effectiveness of your own campaign. A well-run campaign will more than offset any fee that is paid to a qualified consultant. Thus churches should consider using a consultant from a fund-raising organization as a viable option. There are a number of organizations that can be helpful in planning and executing these special campaigns. However, be sure to check out any organization first and ask for references. Both of our organizations, The Malphurs Group at www.malphursgroup.com and Strategic Resources at strategic@lakepointe.org, assist churches in conducting capital campaigns. We will say more about how to conduct capital campaigns in the third section of the book.

Cultivate Giving Champions

A sixth way to develop donors is to cultivate your giving champions. These are people in your church with the gift of giving (Rom. 12:6–8). Rather than ignore them, as many pastors are inclined to do, identify them and meet with them periodically to cultivate their gift along with their relationship with God, just as you might someone with the gift of leadership or evangelism. Ask how the church can minister effectively to them. Do not forget to thank them for their ministry to the church. Make sure that they understand the church's core organizational values, mission, vision, and strategy. There may be times when you will ask them to consider exercising their gift of giving to a particular cause, such as a mission project or a new facility. That is okay. It's the same as when we expect leaders to lead and evangelists to evangelize. Why should we not expect givers to give? When you make that request, it is much better if you do so out of a relationship that you have already developed with your giving champions. They may also help you network with others who have the gift of giving.

We realize that for some people giving attention to key givers is a controversial and questionable idea. Perhaps you are one of those people. However, if we attempt to cultivate the other gifts of our people, why ignore this one? In a *Leadership Journal* article, four pastors were interviewed on how they handle finances in their churches. All four knew who their gifted givers were, and at times asked them for financial help.[6]

Your motives are key to your success. Are your reasons for cultivating your giving champions the right ones? Ask yourself the following questions: Will knowing who our good givers are cause me to favor them over others in the congregation in some way? Am I seeking funds for my personal benefit? Focusing on giving champions is usually more of a controversy in situations of low leadership trust.

To cultivate your giving champions, you must identify them through knowing how much your people give. This is controversial for some pastor-leaders, because it involves their access to the congregation's giving records. If a pastor needs to know who his mature people are, the acid test is likely their giving. Not only is this important information for raising funds but also for raising up leaders, such as board members, staff, and other critical positions.

Many times we have heard pastors say, "I really don't know what any individual in the church gives." Or they might brag to their congregation: "I don't look at the giving records of our people." We think that's a mistake and that such ignorance is dangerous. A pastor cannot develop leaders and he cannot know who to guide into leadership positions if he doesn't know where the hearts of his people are. In Matthew 6:21 the Bible says, "Where your treasure is, there your heart will be also."

Some would say, "I'm afraid that if I know what people are giving, I might favor the wealthy over the ones who don't have as much to give." We don't believe that's the issue. Most pastors already know who are financially wealthy in their congregations. Often you can tell by the cars they drive and the clothes they wear or by their professions. If a pastor were going to be tempted to treat the wealthy better than others, he would already be doing that, with or without knowing specifics about their giving habits. Regardless, if a pastor is concerned about this, he should make it a matter of prayer.

We believe that just as a pastor should know those who have the gift of teaching, the gift of faith, or the gift of leadership, they should know those who have the gift of giving. Years ago I (Steve) established the practice of spending time with some of our large contributors to help them develop their gift of giving. I gave them books on the topic and helped them network with other believers with a more developed gift of giving. This is similar to the way I help some of our teachers develop the gift of teaching or some of our outstanding leaders develop their gift of leadership. Pastors should know and help develop their key givers.

Another way to encourage the gift of giving is to make a point of thanking a person for a key gift. Whenever someone makes a significant gift, I (Steve) make it a point to handwrite a note of thanks to that person. At least once a year I write notes to those who contribute significant amounts on an ongoing basis to thank them for their contribution to our ministry. Also at the end of the year when all the financial records have been compiled, we send a gift of some kind to some of our largest contributors to encourage them in their gift of giving—perhaps a book on stewardship that might help them in their spiritual development or a short DVD that we've put together that reminds them of the lives that have been changed because of their investment. It's somewhat similar to someone who has invested in the stock market. At the end of the year they receive a report on what's been done with their investment and what kind of results have come about because they've chosen to invest in that particular portfolio.

Donor Development Methods

Regularly cast the church's vision

Implement a churchwide stewardship education plan

Constantly communicate with the congregation

Challenge people to make an annual commitment to giving

Conduct capital campaigns

Cultivate giving champions

Questions for Reflection, Discussion, and Application

1. Does your church have a clear, written vision? If it does, do your people understand how their giving has an impact on the vision?

Do you find that in general your people are giving well? If you do not have a written vision, how will you cast a vision that will encourage people to give of their finances to the ministry?

2. Does your church lack any of the seven ways of educating your congregation given in this chapter? Which ones? Would any of these be difficult to implement in your situation? If so, why?

3. Are you good about communicating with your congregation? If not, what is the trust level of your congregation—high or low? How could you communicate regularly with your congregation?

4. Do you have a class or workshop for new members? If so, do you ask them for a commitment to the ministry? Does it include a financial commitment? Why or why not? Do you remind your people at least once a year of their commitment to giving and challenge them in this area? Why or why not?

5. Has your church ever been involved in a capital campaign? Why or why not? If so, what were your giving goals for the campaign? Did you accomplish your goals for the campaign? Why or why not? Would you do it again? Why or why not?

6. Both authors endorse cultivating a church's giving champions (gifted givers). Do you agree or disagree with them? Why? Would you be tempted to give good givers undue preference? What would your people think if they knew their pastor had access to their giving records?

$\mathcal{B}3\mathcal{C}$

Maximizing Contributions

How many ways can people give to your church? Most churches provide only two or three ways for their people to exercise the privilege of giving to the church's ministry for the Savior. The problem is that these churches and their people are missing out on some wonderful opportunities for expanding kingdom giving. There are at least five different ways that people can and will give when provided the opportunity. And all five should be emphasized during the year. Some people refer to them as the "five pockets of giving."

The General Fund

The first pocket is the general fund. This fund is used for such important matters as staff salaries, programming, and facilities (insurance payments, light bills, the mortgage, and such). These are the core items that appear in some form in most church budgets. The general fund isn't very glamorous, but if people don't give to the general fund, the church can't operate and will eventually close its doors. When consulting with struggling churches, especially those in steep decline, we can figure how much longer the church will survive by calculating the rate of decline in worship attendance and the rate of decline in giving to the general fund.

General-fund giving is important to those who care deeply about the church and has an appeal to rule keepers and the rank-and-file who have grown up in the church. The older Builder generation, the people born before 1946, seem the most willing to give to this fund. They understand that money is necessary to run a church, and they're willing to write a check every month without being asked. The obvious question is what happens to Builder-supported churches when the Builder generation moves on to be with their Lord and younger generations have not been taught to give to this fund?

The Building Fund

The second pocket is the building fund. We are amazed at the number of churches with facility needs that do not have a building fund. Many people who give to the general fund will give to the building fund above and beyond their normal giving if a legitimate need is presented to them. There are also some people who will give to the building fund but not to the general fund. They like to see their gift provide something immediate and tangible, and they can conceptualize a building much easier than they can many of the things provided through the general fund.

Because many people will give to a building fund, churches often enter into a one-to-three-year capital campaign during which the church members are asked to give above and beyond their normal giving to provide the down payment for a building or to service a short-term building loan. We will talk more specifically about the details of how to conduct a capital campaign in the latter part of the book.

Some churches work hard at paying off their mortgage and any other debt. Their goal is to become debt free, which often means the elimination of the mortgage on the building plus the elimination of any building fund. The idea seems very noble—they can divert funds from "bricks and mortar" to people and programs. However, the problem with this thinking is that should they have a need to build a facility in the future or acquire more property due to growth, the funds aren't available. They have eliminated one of their primary pockets of giving. And people who may have given to this pocket when they don't give to any of the others invest their money elsewhere, such as in themselves.

We recommend strongly that churches maintain a building fund. We see no problem with keeping debt low or eliminating it if the church's giving is good, but we recommend adding a building fund when churches don't have one and maintaining an existing building fund, even when the building has already been constructed. We also recommend that the portion of the general fund that services debt should not be eliminated.

Getting rid of the building fund will severely limit the church's options in addressing future facility needs. When the money is not currently needed for the building, it can be placed in a savings account for future needs or given on an annual basis to provide facilities for a mission effort, such as a church start.

The Missions Fund

The third pocket of giving is the missions pocket. Once again there are people who will give to missions who won't give to any other fund. They're passionate about God's command to share the gospel around the world, and they're willing to make sacrifices in addition to what they already give to their church to fund a particular mission project or to fund the salaries of missionaries.

While you can find people from most of the generations with this passion, the older Builder generation in particular has been known to be good givers to missions. It's interesting that, while many Builders are quick to write a check to missions, which is good, they're very slow to share the gospel with their neighbor, which is not so good. For them, evangelism is something that takes place overseas and out of sight. The younger adult generation—Busters—are also big givers to missions, primarily because of their personal involvement.

At Lake Pointe we mail out offering envelopes to our church members each month. These envelopes allow for giving to the three pockets—general, building, and missions funds. There's a space to indicate what is being given to the general fund, the building fund, and missions. This allows our people to write one check and then designate on the envelope what portion of that check they want to go to each of these categories. The fact that we have these options on the envelope reminds people of the three pockets. We believe that at Lake Pointe we have people giving to both missions and the building fund who would not normally do so on a regular basis were it not for the opportunity provided by the envelope. Because it is there, we receive substantial offerings in all three of these areas every single week of the year.

The Designated-Giving Fund

We find several examples of designated giving in the New Testament. In Acts 11:27–30 Luke writes that the church in Antioch provided help, or designated an offering, for the church in Jerusalem to see them through a famine. We suspect that, after the disciples in the church at Antioch had given to this collection, they would have been upset if the gift had been used for some other project. Another example of designated giving is the collection of funds for God's people in Jerusalem that Paul mentions in 1 Corinthians 16:1–4.

A Problem

Our experience is that there are many church leaders who are afraid of the designated pocket. They think they know where the church needs to spend its money. They fear that if they open up the door to designated giving, their people will begin to direct gifts to designated projects that may not be priorities in the church's overall strategy. Another fear is that people will divert funds away from the general fund to some pet projects. However, when church leaders don't allow for designated giving, the church misses out on money that may not come in otherwise.

A Solution

The key to the designated pocket is to direct the designated gifts. Tell your people in what particular areas you'll receive these gifts. For example, at least once a quarter, Lake Pointe Church sends out a financial newsletter to all of our church members. Along with other information, it presents a list of designated items that are needed. They include items that range from fifty-dollar Bibles for new Christians to a fifty-thousand-dollar, twenty-one-passenger van—and everything in between. The list encourages people who are passionate about a particular area of the church to give to a specific need and know that their gift has made an immediate difference. For example, someone may be passionate about the youth program in our church, and he may also have a high interest in computers because of his job or hobby. He reads over the list and sees that we need two computers for our youth division that cost fifteen hundred dollars apiece. There's a distinct possibility that God may move this person to write a check for fifteen hundred dollars for one or three thousand dollars for both computers. In this way our church can control designated giving and receive money that the person wouldn't have given to the general fund.

A Helpful Practice

Another practice that has proved helpful at Lake Pointe (which we address in chapter 5 on analyzing the budget) is moving items out of the general budget and onto the designated-giving list. As we review the general budget, we look for areas of people's interests and passion that could be funded if they were designated items. An example might be helping to support a missionary or some short-term mission project. Whereas funds for these needs would naturally flow out of the general budget, we can move them into the designated area, and those who are passionate about these missionaries or the particular mission can designate special gifts to them. This frees up funds in the general budget that would normally have gone to these causes and allows us to divert them to other needs in the general budget. If a church decides not to take the items out of the general budget and someone gives to them as a designated item and the budget is met, there will be an end-of-the-year surplus that can be used for debt retirement or some one-time purchase.

There are times when people will ignore the list of designated items and come up with something on their own. For example, we had a lady offer to give a designated gift for a flagpole. We didn't feel that the church needed a flagpole, so we politely refused the gift. The church can always turn down a designated gift or redirect it. However, not to receive such gifts is to leave money on the table.

Along with the quarterly financial newsletter, we include an individualized statement of what a congregant has given to date. Some people think they are giving much more than they are, or they may think their spouse is giving when he or she isn't. The statement serves to inform them of their actual giving. We also send financial statements to church members who have given absolutely nothing to serve as a reminder to give. Along with that financial statement, we enclose another statement that explains such matters as how the church is audited, its checks and balances for accountability, and several stories of how money is being spent.

An Annual Offering

Every December we receive an "annual offering," which is a type of designated offering. It captures money that people receive as end-of-year bonuses and the income some self-employed or "commission only" employees receive at the end of the year. The church publishes a short list of needs that are funded by this annual offering. Most of the time the items on the list are missions related, although when kicking off a capital campaign, the offering may be used for facilities as well.

The Benevolence Fund

The fifth pocket of giving is the benevolence fund. We find some examples of giving for benevolence in the New Testament. When the church at Antioch provided help for the Jerusalem church to see them through a famine (Acts 11:27–30), not only was this designated giving but it would also fall under the benevolence category. The same is true for the example that we cited above in 1 Corinthians 16:1–4. The funds that believers in the Jerusalem church brought to its leadership, as recorded in Acts 4:32–37, were benevolence funds as well.

An Old Practice and the New Practice

Years ago at Lake Pointe we included the cost of benevolence in our general fund. We set a fixed amount for the fund to help people pay their light bills, provide food for their families, and pay for counseling, childcare, hotel rooms for transients, and other needs.

Later we found that it isn't necessary to include benevolence in the general fund if once a year we take up a separate benevolence offering. We do this on Christmas Eve and have determined that we will use 100 percent of the offering to provide for the benevolent needs of the community throughout the year. Since the Christmas Eve service has become the "second Easter" for many churches in America, we, like many churches, have a large crowd that comes to our church on Christmas Eve, and the money they give to that offering has been enough to fund needs all year. If enough money is not collected in this offering, other benevolent offerings can be taken throughout the year.

Some pastors are hesitant to take up an offering at a service that lots of guests are attending. We have discovered, though, that visitors view a benevolence offering differently than other types of offerings when we explain that we're taking up an offering to help the poor and needy. In fact folks who are unchurched non-Christians gain a greater respect for the church when it uses its funds to help with such needs. So the pastor can push a benevolence offering very hard on such an occasion. We say more about the benevolence offering on Christmas Eve than we do about any other offering. And often we have the non-churched write checks for thousands of dollars and put it in the offering plate for this special fund. As a result, over the last twenty-five years, we've collected enough money in that one offering to respond to all legitimate benevolence needs throughout the year. (In 2005, we received more than two hundred thousand dollars in one offering for benevolence.)

Special Offerings

The benevolence offering falls into the category of what we call "special offerings," which churches take up for needs and opportunities not anticipated in the general budget. The examples cited above from Acts 11:27–30 and 1 Corinthians 16:1–4 would fall under this category. We think there is a legitimate role for special offerings in the overall stewardship plan, but we believe you have to be careful not to take up too many of them. We know of churches that take up an offering for some kind of special project every month. They may do so to provide funds for a particular family whose house burned down or to send a group of people on a mission trip, and so forth. If you're not careful, you'll wear your people out. You'll nickel and dime them to death. What we suggest instead is that you carefully and strategically choose a limited number of special offerings for the year. The benevolence offering is one example. Remember that when it comes to special offerings, less is more! You may be able to help hundreds—if not thousands—of people by taking up a single offering.

A good example of how some churches conduct and perhaps overuse or even abuse special offerings is missions giving. Some churches choose to take up several special missions offerings a year. The church in which I (Steve) grew up, a Baptist church, was such a church. For example, it would take up a state missions offering that would fund missions work around the state for a year. At another time, it would take up a national missions offering that would help fund mission efforts in the continental United States. Then around Christmas it would take up a foreign missions offering. Since the church took other special offerings throughout the year, people felt overwhelmed by it all. It seemed like every time they came to church, they were reaching into their pockets for some worthy cause. Instead of viewing stewardship as a privilege, many were tempted to view it as a burden.

In our church now we give our people the opportunity to give gifts to missions every week of the year because it is one of the options on the offering envelope, and we've chosen to rarely take up special offerings in our worship services throughout the year. That way we're not asking them to give all the time. We're not saying a church should never take up a special offering, just take as few as possible, for example one benevolent offering a year instead of one for each needy family. When we have a guest missionary in, we remind our people that when they give weekly to missions, they are providing the resources to support this individual and others.

In summary, we believe there are far too many churches today that have too few pockets of giving. To balance what we have just stated: More "pockets," less offerings. Consequently, they deny people opportunities to give to the Lord, and they leave money on the table that could have been used for Christ's kingdom. The people in these churches don't give more because the churches don't ask for more. They have not because they ask not.

The Five Pockets of Giving

General Fund

Building Fund

Missions Fund

Designated-Giving Fund

Benevolence Fund

Questions for Discussion, Reflection, and Application

1. How many pockets or opportunities of giving does your church provide for its people? Do they include the five covered in this chapter? If not, why not? Will you add any of these?
2. Do the people in your church prefer to give to a particular fund? If so, which one? Why do you think this is?
3. Does your church take up many special offerings? If so, why? Does this have a positive or negative effect on giving?
4. How does your church handle designated giving? Does it try to control designated funds? If so, how do people react?

Part 2

Managing Your Kingdom Resources

There are several issues related to finances that church leaders must understand. This part of the book covers such topics as developing a strategic budget, deciding how to manage your kingdom resources, checks and balances that must be in place, the annual audit, planning for the future in terms of projected costs and income along with capital campaigns and the cost of buildings and land, dealing with bankers and lending institutions, staff compensation, various legal issues, and church indebtedness.

❧4❧

Developing a Strategic Budget

Before you read any farther, note that the title of this chapter is "Developing a Strategic Budget," not "Developing a Budget." What's the difference? A strategic budget guides the church in allotting and spending its money in congruence with its deep, defining core values to accomplish a specific, biblical mission and a clear, compelling vision. It follows the basics of a good budget but focuses on where God is taking the church.

A budget guides a church in how it will spend its money, but too often it ignores the ministry's values and the plan to accomplish its mission and vision. It may be that the church doesn't even know what its core values are and may not have a biblical mission and a vision. Instead, it allocates funds to keep the doors open, meet salaries, pay the light bill, and so forth. That's just a budget, nothing more. You don't want that! So how can you develop a strategic budget? The answer is the following five-step process.

Step 1: Review Values, Mission, Vision, and Strategy

Step 1 assumes that you have been through some type of strategic envisioning process and that your church has identified the core values that drive it, has articulated a mission and a vision that address its direction, and has a strategy in place to accomplish its mission-vision. And we must add one other item: you—the pastor—and your leaders are excited about all this! Churches that have been through this envisioning process and

53

have done it well have leaders who are so excited about what God is going to do in their communities that they find it difficult to sleep at night.

As we've said above, without a clear vision, values, and a strategy, you'll not be able to develop a strategic budget. It's practically impossible to develop such a budget if you don't know who you are (your values), where you're going (your mission-vision), and how you'll get there (your strategy). At this point you may be thinking, *We've not thought through any of these core issues, and we've always been able to develop a budget in the past. In fact we have one right now.* Allow us to elaborate on what we have said above. Most churches do have a budget, but our experience is that most don't have a strategic budget, and that's a major reason that 80 to 85 percent of the churches in America are plateaued or declining.

Planning your budget involves the ministry's leadership in numerous decisions that are most difficult (if not impossible) to make if you don't know your values, mission, and vision. So if you have not taken this first step, now is the time to do so. If at all possible, put off the budgeting process and do the strategic envisioning (planning) first. Then you'll be able to develop a strategic budget that will provide the financial capital to fuel your future direction and make a difference for Christ in your ministry community.

If it isn't possible to delay planning your budget, go with your current budget and begin the envisioning process as soon as possible. Then you'll be prepared to address the budget later. We suggest that you read Aubrey's book *Advanced Strategic Planning*, 2nd edition, or contact the Malphurs Group (www.malphursgroup.com). They will be able to give you much help in implementing these vital elements.

Step 2: Determine Next Year's Income

The second step in developing a strategic budget is to project how much money the church or ministry anticipates will come in over the next twelve months. Some refer to this as forecasting. This is done in several ways.

Examine Your Giving Track Record

One way to help determine next year's income is looking at the track record of the organization and what the past giving has been (see figure 1). To accurately project future giving, it is important to pay attention to past trends of increases, decreases, or flatline giving from year to year. History is very important because, unless something significant changes in the ministry, the same pattern will likely continue.

Figure 1

Community Church Budget Projection for 2008

Numerical Increase Method

History of Giving		Increase over Previous Year
2004	$300,000	
2005	$450,080	$150,080
2006	$575,000	$124,920
2007	$725,800	$150,800
	Total	$425,800
		÷ 3
		$141,933 average increase
2007 giving	$725,800	
Projected increase	$141,933	
2008 Projected giving	$867,733	

Don't simply increase your budget. Some leaders wrongly assume that they can interrupt and change a downward or level pattern if they set a larger budget amount. They naively believe that somehow, almost magically, people will rise to the occasion to meet the higher goal. We can assure you that increasing the annual budget does not determine what the people will give. And it may anger some.

In calculating a budget trend, it's important to use real giving numbers. Ask, "What was the actual giving over the past three to five years?" This may be a different number than the "approved budget."

When you predict future giving, you want to work with whole numbers not percentages. For example, you may bring in $10,000 the first year and $20,000 the following year. The more important figure is the $10,000 increase not the 100 percent increase. The budget could increase by another $10,000 the next year, bringing it up to $30,000. That's a 50 percent gain the second year, not a 100 percent gain. Using percentages in this case could be misleading.

You want to base all projections on the actual numerical increase in giving each year. For example, your giving is $100,000 one year, and the second year it goes up to $110,000. Then it increases to $120,000 the third year. There's a good chance that it will increase the fourth year to $130,000. What you're looking for is a pattern—a numerical pattern, not a percentage, because a pattern will enable you to project more accurately.

Of course this kind of projecting is difficult if you do not have an extensive giving history. If you are starting a Christian organization or church, and you have only a two-to-three-month history, it's hard to project what you're going to bring in over the next twelve months. When developing a short-term budget with very little giving history, the safest thing is to assume that you'll bring in monthly what you are currently bringing in. Then, as you gain more history and you see, for example, that your giving is increasing by, say, $1,000 a month, you can project that pattern out to the end of the year. Then you can actually come up with a reasonable twelve-month budget.

Consider Your Attendance and Giving Trends

Another way to project your income for the coming year is to observe your attendance trends and per capita giving ratio (see figure 2). How do you compute this? Start with last year's giving record. Let's say it was $450,000. You would divide this by your average worship attendance for last year. If that figure was 450 people, you would divide $450,000 by 450 people. The result would be your yearly per capita giving—$1,000. You might think that this figure is very low. However, in 2002 per capita giving in the average growing church in America was around $767[1] Our research shows that a good benchmark for a church is around $1,000 per person per year.

Let's push this a little further. If you know that your average attendance is growing by 100 people every year, then you can predict that next year's average attendance is going to be 550 people. If you assume your per capita giving is going to be exactly the same next year—$1,000 per person per year—then your expected income would be $550,000.

To be more accurate, you could also look to see if there is a trend of increases in your per capita number. Use your weekly per capita figure because it will be more accurate (some months have five weeks). To find this, take your per capita annual giving, in this case $1,000, and divide it by 52 weeks. This means your per capita weekly giving is $19. If you look at the church's history, and two years ago you had a $17–weekly per capita giving, the following year you had an $18–weekly per capita giving, and this year you have a $19–weekly per capita giving, it's safe to say that you're not only going to increase your attendance by an average of 100 people, but that your weekly per capita giving will increase by $1 a person to $20 per person per week.

If you look at the history of the church, and two years ago you had a $34–weekly per capita giving, the following year you had a $36–weekly per capita giving, and this year you have a $38–weekly per capita, it's safe to say that you're not only going to increase your attendance by an average of 100 people, but that your weekly per capita giving will increase by $2 a person.

There are two other important factors to address before we leave this second way to project your income. The first factor is the formula and the figures you use. It's important that your formula for figuring your per capita giving uses the same numbers from year to year. Be consistent. It doesn't really matter what you count, as long as the numbers are accurate and that you're using the same measure.

The second factor addresses whom you count. Some churches count all the people who are in the children's church as well as the auditorium. Others count only the people in the auditorium. It doesn't really matter. Your per capita giving obviously is going to be higher if you count only the adults, but as long as you're using the same number each year, you can make a good projection.

Figure 2

Projected Attendance × Projected Per Capita Method

Year	Average Attendance	Increase	Giving	Per Capita		Increase
2004	291		$300,000	$1,031	÷ 52 = $19.83	
2005	382	91	$450,080	$1,178	÷ 52 = $22.65	$2.82
2006	471	89	$575,600	$1,222	÷ 52 = $23.50	$ .85
2007	553	82	$725,800	$1,312	÷ 52 = $25.23	$1.73
Total		262	Total increases			$5.40
		÷ 3				÷ 3
	Average Increase 87		Average increase			$1.80

2007 attendance	553
+ projected average increase	87
Projected 2008 average attendance	640

2007 per capita giving	$25.23/week
+ projected per capita increase	1.80
2008 projected per capita giving	$27.03/week
	x 52
	$1,406 per capita per year

2008 projected average attendance	640
2008 projected annual per capita giving	1,406
2008 projected giving	$899,840

Compare Both Methods

We recommend that you use both methods (see figure 3). First, examine your church's total income record. Then consider your attendance trends and per capita giving. Once you have these two figures, compare them. Are they close? Another approach would be to combine the two methods. Add them together and divide by two. The result is a third way to project next year's income.

Figure 3

Combine Both Methods

Numerical increase projection for 2008	$867,733
Per Capita Projection	899,840
	$1,767,573
	÷ 2
2008 projected giving average	$ 883,787

Step 3: Determine the Allocation of Funds

The third step in developing a strategic budget is to determine the allocation of funds. There are numerous ways to accomplish this. We will present two of the better approaches: the fundamentals approach and the functions approach.

The Fundamentals Approach

The fundamentals approach allocates funds to four fundamental areas (or allocation pockets): missions, personnel, programming, and facilities. We use the term *fundamentals* because these four areas are fundamental to most budgeting systems, and the budget has to address these areas in some way for a church to operate. We like the fundamentals approach. It's how we allocate funds at Lake Pointe, and it has worked extremely well for us, helping us address the delicate balance between evangelism and edification as we pursue our mission and vision.

Missions

The first fundamental in the budget is missions. Most churches realize the importance of and the need to support missions to some extent. A church needs to support both missions and local evangelism.

We believe that a church that desires biblical, numerical growth along with spiritual health will allocate about 10 percent of its budget for missions. The church should develop missions policies that govern whom they support, under what circumstances, and how much they give. In addition, the church should spell out its expectations and how it will know if its missionaries are being effective. Biblical stewardship demands an accounting (see Matt. 25:14–30). And this will help the church ensure that the money they budget for missions is being put to its best use for Christ's kingdom.

Personnel

The second budgeting fundamental is personnel, which is the largest allocation of funds in most budgets. We recommend that the church designate about 50 percent of its budget for its personnel. Often in large churches it can be a little less (45–50 percent) and in small churches a little more (50–55 percent).

Why so much? People are God's human agents for ministry effectiveness (1 Cor. 3:5–9). God prefers to accomplish his purposes through people (Phil. 2:13) and then blesses them in return. Your ministry will be only as good as the people who serve the Lord and the church. Scripture is clear that the worker (in this context, likely, the first-century pastors) deserves his wages (1 Tim. 5:17–18). In fact Paul says here that those who lead well and preach and teach are worthy of double honor. It is not only unbiblical but shameful when a church that has the means fails to take care of its staff.

To use its funds wisely, the church should have personnel policies in place that address staff finances. These should establish the base salary for various positions. There should also be policies concerning raises. For example, are cost-of-living raises automatic? Are raises based strictly on performance? We tackle these policies in chapter 10 where we discuss paying staff.

Programming

A church must pay careful attention to its programming, because this is how it serves God and the people who attend its ministries. Programming also has a major impact on fundraising as people contribute through the various church ministries. We recommend that a church put approximately 20 percent of its funding into this vital area. It is important to note that almost everything that is not missions, personnel, or facilities falls into this category. Such items as copiers, paper supplies, stamps, and so forth all go to support the church's programming. Some have labeled this area as "miscellaneous" or "other" instead of programming.

A major part of programming is what we refer to as the church's primary and secondary ministry activities, along with any age-group or age-related ministries. A church's primary activities are those ministries that are crucial to the accomplishment of its mission and vision, the ministries that all members and attenders must be involved in if they are to become mature believers. These are ministries like the worship-preaching service, Sunday school, or small groups. A church's secondary activities are those elective ministries that serve to support or complement in some way the primary ministries, such as vacation Bible school and men's and women's ministries. (Aubrey covers these more in depth in chapter 8 of *Advanced Strategic Planning*.) The church's age-related or age-specific ministries are made up of these primary and secondary activities.

The church will focus on funding its primary activities first because they are so key to making mature disciples, and some of them, such as the worship service, provide the greatest funding in return. In terms of ROI (return on investment), the worship service provides for much of the church's income and may fund the rest of the primary, as well as many of the secondary, ministry activities.

In allocating funds for programming, the church needs to consider its people's expectations. Some people believe that, because they support the church financially, it should provide them with Sunday school supplies, free child care, and the materials needed in various programs.

Facilities

Well-meaning church planters will often start out their ministries with the idea that they will invest in people rather than bricks and mortar. This means that they do not plan to purchase or build a facility. Their plan is to rent what they need and put the rest back into recruiting and securing competent staff and ministering to the people. While this sounds great, unfortunately, it seldom works quite that way. We suspect that one reason is our culture. People want a place they can identify with and call their own ("our church"). They also grow weary of all the disadvantages of not owning their own building, such as unclean facilities and the hassle of setting up and taking down chairs and tables, sound systems, and nursery furniture. The bottom line is that most churches eventually want a permanent facility.

We advise churches to allocate between 20 and 25 percent of funding for their facilities. Primarily this includes a mortgage payment, insurance, and utilities. Some churches will pay off their mortgage and divert those funds to another part of the budget. As we explained in chapter 3, we do not recommend that a church do this.

If you have a mortgage that is paid off, you may be able to allocate a lower percentage to facilities. But we warn churches that if they know they have a building need coming up in the future—even if their mortgage is paid off—they need to have a sufficient percentage of their general

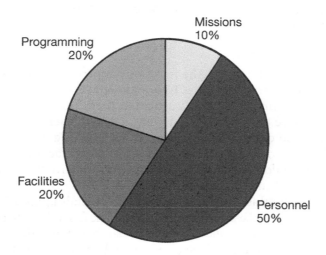

fund allocated to service future mortgage payments. If you do not have a current building payment, that money can go into a building fund to provide a down payment for a future building. More important than that, it will provide a steady stream of income that can help service any future mortgage debt. Once you decrease the slice of the pie set aside for facilities to increase monies for personnel or programming, it's most difficult to get that allocation back to provide for facility needs. Then you're stuck with having to pay cash for all future buildings and having to raise 100 percent of needed funds through a capital campaign, because there's no funding mechanism left in your general fund to service any mortgage loans.

We've found that these are general allocations for a healthy church. Is there room for some variation? The answer is yes. These percentages can shift during certain seasons of ministry. For example, if you have a capital campaign in progress that includes facilities, you may be able to budget less of your general fund for building needs.

The Functions Approach

There are other approaches, besides the fundamentals approach, to the allocation of a church's funds, but most are modifications to fit a church's individual situation. However, another approach that we think you should consider is what we refer to as the functions approach. I (Aubrey) have encouraged my students at Dallas Seminary to consider this approach, and I've come across a few churches that have used it or a modified form of it. This is also the approach Rick Warren endorses (however, he uses the term *purpose* rather than *function*). Here is a brief overview of the functions approach.

Allocation of Funds

As is clear from its name, the functions approach allocates funds to the church's ministry functions. To implement this approach, a church has to identify it functions, clearly articulate them, and vigorously pursue them. We believe that, according to Acts 2:42–47, there are at least five functions of the church: evangelism, Bible teaching, fellowship, worship, and service or ministry. Thus, if a church embraces this allocation approach, it would allocate funds directly to these five functions rather than to the four fundamentals.

If you compare this approach to the fundamentals approach, you will see the need to ask some important questions. The first relates to personnel: where do you place your allocations to personnel? Since this is a fundamental allocation for all budgets, it has to appear somewhere. With this approach you would list personnel under each function and allocate funds accordingly. The same would hold for the fundamentals of programming and facilities. However, a potential problem is allocating funds to facilities, since facilities would come under each function. Some address this by using a modified approach, allocating funds to the church's ministry functions but also allocating funds to certain fundamentals, such as facilities. Thus their budget includes both functions and certain fundamentals.

Strengths and Weaknesses

Like any other approach, this one has both strengths and weaknesses. The strength of this approach is that it focuses attention on ministry by emphasizing the church's functions. A weakness, however, is its complexity. It spreads some fundamentals, like facilities, over four or five allocation pockets, rather than putting them in one category, which is far simpler.

Step 4: Communicate Allocations

The fourth step is to communicate to your paid and lay leadership the approximate amount of money they will have to spend for their areas of ministry. Once you've anticipated your income for the coming year and determined how to allocate that income (what portion of the pie is going to each major area), then you should communicate the decisions to your paid staff and lay leadership. When they have an idea of approximately how much money they have to spend, it frees them to plan their coming year and submit budget requests that stay within basic allocation parameters.

Uncontrollable Expenses

When communicating the allocation of the coming year's income to various ministries, be careful to hold some money in reserve for uncontrollable expenses, because there will always be expenses over which you have little or no control. Health insurance for church employees may go up 20 percent in one year when the general budget increases by only 10 percent. The same might happen with postage or utilities. If you expect revenue to increase 10 percent, you can't give everyone a 10 percent increase, because it may be necessary for some items to increase more than others. And if you give everyone the full percentage allocation that the entire budget is projected to increase, there will be no money left over for one-time-expense requests or ministry-expansion requests. So when you allocate funds, be sure to allow disproportionate increases in some areas.

Advantages of Communication

There are several advantages to communicating the allocations. First, letting everyone know beforehand what their allocation is helps them keep their budget requests within reason. Second, it prevents a central board or senior staff from making draconian cuts in the requests of a ministry they know little about. Third, this model eliminates the temptation of a board or senior person to micromanage a ministry's spending, and instead empowers staff and volunteers to determine how to spend their allocation in line with their strategy. (The authority to spend money on ministry should come with the responsibility for leading that ministry.) Fourth, communicating to each ministry their funding allocation empowers them to plan intelligently.

Communicating allocations to ministry leaders should make good sense because it works in the same way that most people manage their personal finances. For example, they don't dream up what kind of house they'd like to live in or what kind of car they'd like to have or where they'd like to go on vacation and submit their dreams to their boss, asking for a salary increase. The boss tells them what their salary is, and then—and only then—should they determine what kind of car they're going to drive, what kind of house they're going to live in, and where they're going on vacation. You help the leaders of your ministry areas by telling them what their financial parameters will be and then ask them to work within them and spend well in terms of developing their own strategic budgets.

The various ministries still submit budget requests to a central body for review and approval; however, that body shouldn't have to adjust the allocations except in rare situations. The only decisions the central budget committee or senior staff have to make should be one-time requests and ministry-expansion requests (see below under Establish Baselines). And those decisions are made based on available funds and ministry priorities.

Grassroots Spending

We want to amplify the concept of allowing the people who have to lead and carry out a particular ministry the freedom to determine how funding for their ministry is spent. For example, the church has charged the youth pastor with the responsibility of reaching young people for Christ and then discipling them. Some finance committee or supervisor should not tell him, "You can't spend money on soft drinks; we'd rather you spent the money on Bibles." This is ministry and financial micromanaging. Instead, the supervisor should tell the youth pastor what his job expectations are and how much money he has in his budget. Then the supervisor lets the youth pastor determine how he'll use the available resources to accomplish the ministry. If he doesn't lead the ministry well and manages the funds poorly, then the supervisor, not a budget or finance committee, must step in and address the situation. If others get involved in the process, the youth pastor ends up with multiple supervisors, which is a formula for ministry and fiscal disaster.

Unfortunately many ministries reverse the proper order. They ask their paid and lay leaders to dream big dreams for God, determine the programming to make these dreams a reality, and then request the finances necessary to accomplish the vision. Leaders and their staff become excited over the prospect of seeing their dreams become a reality, but their dreams are dashed when someone from the finance committee tells them that the church is unable to provide the requested funds.

Zero-Based Budgeting

Some financial experts advocate zero-based budgeting. This is when every year those making the budget start over, and the previous year's allocations have no bearing on future allocations. The experts argue that zero-based budgeting eliminates "budget barnacle" expenditures. Budget barnacles are those expenditures that have become routine over the years and that no one challenges, even though they should be challenged. Like barnacles, they attach themselves to the budget ship, and while they may go relatively unnoticed, they have an effect. They slow the ship down as it steams toward its mission port.

In most cases, once an item makes it into the budget, the chances are slim that it will be removed when it's no longer needed. The way to address this is not to start all over, as in zero-based budgeting, but to have supervisors review the budget allocations line by line, asking for a justification of each line item. If an expenditure cannot be justified, it should be eliminated. In some rare cases, the allocation may just need to be cut back.

Establish Baselines

While zero-based budgeting sounds good—and you certainly want to eliminate any expenditures that don't produce the goals of a particular ministry—there must be a baseline from which every ministry has to operate. If you tell the individual ministry leader the amount of money he or she has to work with for the coming year and then ask him or her to come up with a budget that stays within that amount, you establish a baseline and save the ministry leader much time and effort. When other legitimate needs arise, the leader can always request more resources.

There are two ways that a ministry leader can request more resources. First, the ministry leader could request a *one-time expenditure*. For example, you might ask your youth pastor to submit a general budget for the youth area for forty-two thousand dollars. However, if he finds this to be inadequate because the youth need a big-screen television for their activities center, the leader can submit a one-time-expenditure request. Such a request is used for an allocation that is needed for the coming year but won't be needed in subsequent years. Therefore it doesn't become a permanent part of the budget. Otherwise there would be additional but unwarranted funds in the youth budget for the following year.

Another way to pursue more resources is the *ministry-expansion request*. For example, the youth pastor decides that he is going to start a new ministry for delinquent kids that cannot be done within the budget allocation for the year. If the central budget committee or senior staff believe in the priority of this new ministry and if funds are available, they can grant the leader additional monies for ministry expansion, rather than asking him to finance the expanded ministry through the existing budget. If granted, the ministry-expansion allocation will become a permanent part of the youth general budget in subsequent years.

Step 5: Set Up a Cash-Forward Reserve

The fifth step is to set up a cash-forward reserve or savings account on deposit with the bank. This is a set amount you would keep with a bank as insurance in case there is a disruption of contributions to the church over one or more Sundays. This might be due to bad weather, a natural disaster, or some economic disaster that would affect contributions in a substantial way. Establishing a cash-forward reserve is the proverbial "saving for a rainy day." When a church establishes such a reserve, it has created margin.

Many churches will keep in a cash-forward reserve the money that would be needed to cover from two weeks to one month of income to ensure liquidity during summer months or during times of decline in giving. The church needs to make sure that it places this money in an interest-bearing account so that it's not losing value because of inflation.

A viable alternative to a cash-forward reserve is a line of credit that you negotiate with the bank. This works much like a credit card. If there is a substantial fluctuation in the church's giving patterns, a line of credit allows you to do some short-term borrowing at predetermined rates to provide short liquidity.

Developing a Strategic Budget

Step 1: Review the church's values, mission, vision, and strategy

Step 2: Determine next year's income

Step 3: Determine the allocation of funds

Step 4: Communicate allocations to paid and lay leadership

Step 5: Set up a cash-forward reserve with a bank

Questions for Reflection, Discussion, and Application

1. Does your church know what its core values are? Why or why not? Does your church have a clear mission statement? Does it communicate the mission statement? Why or why not? Does your church have a dynamic, inspiring vision? Why or why not? Does your church have a strategy to accomplish the mission and vision? Why or why not?

2. If the answer to any or all of the above questions is no, what will you do about this? If you don't do anything, how can you possibly make strategic decisions that affect the future of your church?

3. Of the ways the authors suggest to forecast your income, which would work best for your church? Why?

4. The authors provide you with two approaches to help you allocate funds—the fundamentals approach and the functions approach. Do you find these helpful? Why or why not? Do you have various

allocations in your current budget that don't seem to fit one of the approaches? If so, where will you place them?

5. Does our argument for allocating funds to staff, rather than asking them to request an amount, make sense? Why or why not? How are you deciding on allocations now? Is it working?

6. Is your cash flow such that you could set up a cash-forward reserve with your bank? Is so, does this make sense to you? If not, would it be wise for you to negotiate a line of credit with your bank? Why wouldn't you do this?

Analyzing Your Strategic Budget

Chapter 4 provided you with much information on how to develop a strategic budget. We have written this chapter to help you know how to analyze the budget you develop. Once you've developed your strategic budget according to our suggestions, you would be wise to analyze or evaluate your budget at least annually. This process will tell you how well you are you doing, if your budget is strategic, and if you are wasting any funds. Some tips for doing such an analysis follow.

Compare Budget Allocations

In analyzing your budget, ask, *How do our budget allocations compare to the suggestions of the authors?* In chapter 4 we said we prefer allocating funds in the following manner.

Funding Allocations

Missions	10%
Programming	20%
Personnel	50%
small churches	50–55%
large churches	45–50%
Facilities	20%

This is based largely on how growing, spiritually healthy churches allocate their funds in general. We say "in general" because there will always be some variation, so you need not view this legalistically. Of course the problem is always how much you take from Peter to pay Paul. And Peter would say, "How much will you rob Peter to pay Paul?" The point is that when we make room for variations, somebody gives up something. Who will that be and who makes the decision?

How do your budget allocations compare to ours? Were they close or far apart? Initially you may have struggled somewhat with what goes where. For example, do the utilities go under facilities or programming? If you find that your budget is fairly close to ours, you're doing well, and likely this reflects good giving on the part of your congregation. This has been our experience with most of the churches with which we consult.

You may find that your budget allocations aren't even close to ours. For example, if you're in a building program, you may have placed more funding under facilities. If your church is a strong supporter of missions, you may have more money under missions. If your church is strongly inward-focused, you may have allocated more funding for programming.

If your allocations aren't close to ours, you have some work to do if you desire to bring your allocations in line with those of spiritually healthy, biblically balanced churches. It may seem strange for us to restrict the missions allocation to 10 percent; however, if considerably more is allocated (say, 20 percent or more), there will not be sufficient funds for one, some, or all of the other areas. You may wonder what you can do to fix your budget. A part of the answer is found back in chapter 4 concerning who makes the funding decisions. If you're not a person in the ministry who has power to make funding decisions or at least influence those who do, you may not be able to do anything.

Another possibility is that your situation is temporary. For example, if you're in a remodeling or new building mode, you may have allocated more funds to facilities. However, when the work is done you can readjust the facilities allocation to reflect our recommended allocation. Sometimes budget allocations reflect church politics. For example, a sizeable but vocal minority of congregants may work hard to make sure that their favorite charity or local parachurch ministry receives a significant allocation of funds. And you may have come to the church long after this decision was made. Should you work to change or redirect the allocation? We think that you should, but you would be wise to count the cost. It's essential to be in a ministry long enough to have developed substantial congregational trust before trying to make such a change. If they don't trust you, you can't lead them. Though we tend to think the best time to act is now, you may want to give yourself a little more time to build credibility before you push for this kind of change.

One more bit of advice: choose your battles wisely. A way to do this in analyzing allocations is to ask, *Is this enough money to warrant going to war?* For a few dollars, war is probably not warranted, but for thousands, it may be. You must be wise as serpents and harmless as doves.

Supporting a Biblical Mission and Vision

In analyzing your budget, ask, *Does our budget support a biblical mission and vision?* This assumes that you have both a mission and a vision and that they are biblical. In chapter 4 we advised you that if you don't have a mission and a vision that are clear, compelling, and biblical, you should address this need as soon as possible.

Because your church is in existence, it does have a mission, but is it a biblical mission? According to the Savior, your mission was determined some two thousand years ago. It's the Great Commission found in Matthew 28:19–20 and Mark 16:15, as well as several other places. Our experience is that some evangelical churches' missions aren't necessarily the Great Commission. For example, in some churches there is heavy emphasis on good Bible teaching. And there's nothing wrong with this as long as it doesn't become the church's mission and sole reason for existence. I (Aubrey) have a background in the Bible church movement, and my experience has been that some of the more traditional Bible churches have made good Bible teaching their mission instead of the Great Commission. The result is that in some of these churches evangelism is practically nonexistent.

Your budget will support your church's direction whatever that may be. The hope is that your church's mission is the Great Commission and that your vision and ministries reflect this. Then, most likely, your budget aligns well with this direction. However, if your mission is something other than the Great Commission, your budget will reflect that mission. Here's the key thing to remember: your vision in general and your mission in particular will align with and promote your budget. They will encourage people to support financially the church and its direction. Our concern for your church is that you have the right mission and vision.

A Biblically Balanced Set of Core Values

Next you should ask, *Does our budget reflect a biblically balanced set of core values?* We assume that you know your church's core ministry values. If this isn't the case, you would be wise to determine what they are as soon as possible. Aubrey has written two books—*Values-Driven Leadership*[1] and *Advanced Strategic Planning*—that will help you understand the values concept and discover your actual ministry core values.

We stated above that your church has a direction. It may not be a biblical direction, but it will be taking you somewhere. Your church also has a set of core ministry values, and you must consider whether they are biblical values and if each receives proper attention. They could be biblical values that aren't balanced. You must discover your church's core values and then compare them with those of a biblically functioning, spiritually balanced church. One example of such a church is the church at Jerusalem. In Acts 2:42–47 Luke identifies the church's core ministry values. In this text there are at least five values: biblical teaching, worship, fellowship, service, and evangelism. It isn't easy to determine if your values are receiving appropriate focus. You could ask some of your leaders, such as the board members, if they think the core ministry values receive proper attention. What's the general consensus? If some don't believe there is a balanced focus, do they point to a value (or values) that needs more emphasis?

We assume that your church's values are balanced, like those of the Jerusalem church. Whether or not this is true, your budget will support your church's core values, so it's important that they be the right values. You should ask, *How well does our budget fund biblical teaching, worship, fellowship, service, and evangelism?* As you look over your budget, are any of these areas missing altogether or funded poorly? And how can you know? Again, our recommended budget allocations in the first tip above and in chapter 4 will help you determine this. However, the circumstances of every church are different, so the budget recommendations we make are flexible.

Budget Orientation

Ask, *Is our budget outreach or in-reach oriented?* In-reach ministries focus primarily on believers and provide for their needs. Outreach activities focus on unbelievers and their needs. Both are important and both are addressed in Christ's Great Commission.

As much as possible, a good strategic budget emphasizes both in-reach and outreach allocations. We must budget for both outreach and in-reach, but the allocations won't be equal because the activities for in-reach usually require more funds than those for outreach. Surprisingly, it doesn't take a lot of money to support an outreach-oriented strategy. Facilities and personnel can be used for either outreach or in-reach, so you can't always quantify the emphasis by looking only at the budget numbers.

Not all outreach ministries will be found under a specific budget item marked "evangelism." Some of your in-reach ministries may serve to reach out as well. An example might be a worship service. God is so present in some worship services that unbelievers go away having sensed that he was there, as in 1 Corinthians 14:24–25. Another example is ministry personnel who lead what are commonly viewed as in-reach ministries. These people may have a gift and/or a passion for evangelism. Thus they'll look for opportunities to budget and use their in-reach ministries to promote evangelism and outreach. Finally, if you have a pastor of evangelism or a pastor of assimilation, as some larger churches do, the budget allocation for these positions will be under personnel and not evangelism and missions. So be aware of items in the budget that promote outreach but are under different categories in the budget.

Giving That Is Growing, Plateaued, or in Decline

You don't have to be a rocket scientist to know that often a church's giving reflects its attendance and fuels its budget. Ask, *Are our church's income and budget increasing, plateaued, or declining?* What does the answer say about your church? Churches that are growing in attendance find their income is growing, while most churches that are declining in attendance find their income declining as well. And both have a profound impact on the budget, whether positive or negative.

However, I (Aubrey) have found in some plateaued and declining churches that for awhile the income increases rather than decreases, as might be expected. Several years ago I worked with a Southern Baptist church in west Texas where this was the case. I suspect that in churches like this, some people—most likely the older Builder generation—have adopted the value of giving but not the value of evangelism. This pattern cannot be sustained.

Per Capita Giving

Next ask, *What is our average per capita per annum giving?* For the sake of comparison, in 2002 per capita giving for the average growing church in America was around $767.[2] Our research indicates that a good benchmark for a church is approximately $1,000 per person per annum, which is $83.33 per month and $19.23 per week. The following may help you determine whether your church is close to the average nationwide.

Your actual income will depend on your church's constituency—the income of your people, as well as where the church is located in the world. In addition, a church of one hundred people that is struggling spiritually will likely give less than a church of the same size that is spiritually strong. To get a good idea of average giving, simply divide the budget by the number of people in attendance. Likely you will know approximately what your people earn, so compare the two. It will be less if you are ministering in the inner city, targeting young people, or are seeker-targeted (new believers tend to give less than established believers).

Average Worship Attendance	Annual Giving
50 people	$ 50,000
100 people	$ 100,000
200 people	$ 200,000
500 people	$ 500,000
1000 people	$1,000,000
2000 people	$2,000,000
5000 people	$5,000,000

Some people are shocked at our using a benchmark of $1,000 per capita per annum, especially when they minister in middle-class, white-collar, educated congregations. They think this figure is too low. But it reflects reality. Most people, even affluent people, give little to their churches. Usually this has to do with the spiritual condition and growth of the church. People do not support struggling churches that have little or no vision. At the same time, most people agree that churches should aim for more than $1,000 per person.

Whether or not one believes that tithing is for today, it was certainly a measure of what good giving was in the Old Testament. Thus it can also serve as a benchmark for good giving today. So if we consider average giving is around $1,000 per capita per annum (or $2,000 per household with two adults), that would represent a tithe of a $20,000–income. Does that reflect the income of most of your church members?

Other Means of Funding

Ask, *Are there ministries that should be financed by means other than the general fund?* A fund can be created that is designated for special projects; the staff or board would have the authority to use such a fund on unexpected opportunities or time-sensitive needs.

Another alternative funding method is to provide a list of projects or expenditures that people can give to, such as camp scholarships. An example at Lake Pointe is the benevolence fund we described in an earlier chapter. Unlike most churches, Lake Pointe does not include benevolence in their general budget. We take up a one-time offering for benevolence at our Christmas service. Next to Easter, our Christmas service is our best attended meeting of the year, and many of these people are unchurched unbelievers who live in the area. We announce that we will take up an offering and that it's for benevolence. Most of the people in attendance like the fact that we're not after their money for general budget expenditures but to help needy people in the community.

Another way to provide additional funds is what we refer to as "user costs." User costs are items that are often funded by the church's budget, but people should be paying for them out of their pockets. We have observed that when people give to their church, they expect certain things in return. It amounts to a church social security system. They give but they want something back. And this is so subtle that most people aren't even aware of it. For example, people expect free Sunday school supplies (such as quarterly women's and men's Bible study materials) and childcare at all activities.

We believe that when people give to God through the church, they should not have self-serving expectations. If they do, we believe they've missed what giving should be about. We give to God because of all that he's done for us in grace. We don't give to God with a spirit of entitlement. Therefore, we suggest that the church ask their people to pay for some items, such as Sunday school quarterlies, Bible study booklets, and similar items. We also believe that when people pay for certain items, they value them more and take better care of them.

Inappropriate Funding

Ask, *Are there items in our budget that the church should not be funding?* Go line by line through the entire budget, and ask about each item: *Why is the church funding this?* As we said earlier, while it's often difficult to get an item or ministry into the church's budget, once it's there, it's even more difficult to remove it. Even the missions budget should be questioned. This helps the church determine how its money is being used and whether it is putting its money into ministries that are truly making a difference for the Savior.

Sometimes you may identify an item that belongs in the budget but is in the wrong place. This may not seem important, but it could throw your allocation process off significantly, depending on the item. For example, I (Aubrey) was consulting with one church when I noted an individual's name listed under the missions budget. When I questioned this item, the pastor explained that he was a former pastor and this was the way the church was attempting to provide for his retirement. My advice was to move this expenditure to personnel so that it would not be part of the missions allocation.

High- and Low-Cost Items

The next question is, *What high- and low-cost items are in the budget?* Often the primary ministry activities that do the most to accomplish the church's mission cost less to support than the secondary activities. Thus you may want to reevaluate some of the more costly secondary activities. Are they effective enough to warrant being in the budget? Could you replace them with other equally effective ministries that would cost less?

Keep in mind that often the primary ministries, such as the preaching-worship service, bring in the most return on investment. Also they are critical to the church's fulfilling the Great Commission. So you want to make sure that your church's primary ministry activities are fully funded, because a breakdown here could affect the church's disciple-making process.

Denominational Support

Ask, *Are we getting our money's worth from our denominational support?* You may want to evaluate any money that your church may have budgeted for its denomination.

We live and minister in a time when a growing number of younger Christians are questioning denominational support and loyalty. They don't understand the reason for being a part of a denomination. Because many denominations do not have the authority to determine how much a church must allot for denominational support, many assume a defensive posture, having to justify their existence and fighting for their survival.

Lake Pointe is Southern Baptist by heritage, but we would never support our denomination simply because it is expected. We monitor where our denomination is doctrinally, what it's doing to make a difference for the kingdom, and how it's helping churches be the very best they can be for Christ. Even though we still support our denomination financially, we find we are redirecting some money, which before would have flowed through the denomination, to give direct support to missions and world causes. This allows us to support, with a group of churches, our denomination's efforts, while at the same time supporting ministries that are particularly meaningful to our own church.

Your Church's Expectations

Finally, ask, *How high are our expectations of our people in terms of giving?* The general rule is the more you expect, the more you'll get. At Lake Pointe our budget has finished in the black for twenty-six consecutive years. And some of those years it has been as much as one million dollars over budget. We believe that there are two reasons. The leadership, including the pastor and elder board, have provided a clear vision for the church, and they hold high biblical expectations for the people in terms of their giving.

Church members are informed when they join that all church members are expected to support the church financially in a God-honoring manner, and they are asked to sign a commitment to do so at the new member orientation.

Analyzing Your Strategic Budget

How do your budget allocations compare with the suggestions of the authors?

Does your budget support a biblical mission and vision?

Does your budget reflect a biblically balanced set of core values?

Is your budget outreach or in-reach oriented?

Are your church's income and budget increasing, plateaued, or declining?

What is your church's average per capita per annum giving?

Are there ministries that should be financed by means other than the general fund?

Are there items in your budget that the church should not be funding?

What high- and low-cost items are in the budget?

Is your church getting its money's worth from your denominational support?

How high are your church's expectations for your people in terms of giving?

Questions for Reflection, Discussion, and Application

1. As you asked and thought through the questions in this chapter, were you pleased or displeased with your church's budget? Why? If you are displeased, what will you do about it?
2. Based on the analysis, what pleased or excited you the most about your church's budget? Why? What about it pleased you the least or may have even discouraged you? Why?
3. Which tip proved most helpful to your situation? Why? Which proved least helpful to your situation? Why?
4. Did applying any of these tips free up funding for more important ministry? If so, which ones? If not, why not?

৯৬৫

Deciding Who Decides

How does your church decide where it will invest its financial resources? That's a power question. And the answer depends on who has power in the church along with the authority to exercise that power. Power resides in every church. How should the local church handle its power as it seeks to influence people for God?

A church's answer to the power question affects how that church spends its money. This chapter begins by addressing how various churches answer the power question. It wrestles with who should have the power. It looks at two biblical principles that address power and provides two scenarios for the distribution of power. Finally, it presents an example of how one church has implemented a congregation-ruled, board-led, and staff-managed approach to power and how that affects its finances.

The Church's Relationship to Power

The answer to how the local church should handle its power is found in the church's polity. Polity concerns whom the church empowers. The church has wrestled with this issue of power in one way or another since the first century. Three major types of church polity or government have surfaced over the years: episcopal, presbyterian, and congregational.

The Bishops Have the Power

The episcopal form of polity or government is hierarchical, placing the power to influence in the hands of bishops. It is primarily the Methodist, Orthodox, Anglican, Episcopal, and Roman Catholic churches that practice this polity. Most of these churches follow a threefold ministry hierarchy in the church, exercised by bishops, presbyters, and deacons. There has been an attempt to trace this authority back to the apostles (apostolic succession).

Only the bishops have the power to consecrate other bishops and ordain priests and deacons. Thus the bishops hold the power in this system and would strongly influence their churches' handling of finances. The problem for some of these churches is that not only do the bishops operate outside the church, but they often preside over a significant number of churches. Thus they may have little knowledge of the local church's situation in general and its financial needs in particular.

Is this polity supported by Scripture? There is biblical support for presbyters or elders as well as deacons (1 Tim. 3:1–10 and other passages). However, the office of bishop appears to be the same as the office of elder, not a separate office with superior power over the others, so the episcopal form, in our opinion, has little biblical support.

The Elders Have the Power

The presbyterian form of polity is federal. It places the power to influence in the hands of certain leaders, often called elders. A number of churches that practice this polity are governed by a session that is composed of two kinds of elders—ruling and teaching elders. The ruling elders are laymen that are elected by the congregation. They assist in the government of the church. The teaching elder is the pastor or minister who is ordained by other ministers. The teaching elder is responsible to minister the Word and sacraments to the church. There are variations of this format, such as a board of lay elders with one elder who serves as a teaching elder. It is primarily Presbyterian and Reformed groups, as well as some independents and Bible churches, that practice this polity. Most hold that both classes of elder are equal and have equal authority in the church.

Is this approach biblical? There is ample scriptural support for this view. Elders are involved as leaders throughout the New Testament (Acts 11:30; 14:23; 15:2, 22; 20:17; Titus 1:5; James 5:14; 1 Peter 5:1). In 1 Timothy 5:17 Paul refers to the elders at Ephesus who "direct the affairs of the church." They are "worthy of double honor, especially those whose work is preaching and teaching." Apparently some ruled, and some who ruled also taught. However, this is probably a reference to the city church made up of these elders who were likely the pastors of house churches located all over Ephesus. Some would also use 1 Thessalonians 5:12–13 and Hebrews 13:17 to argue that congregants should submit to the elders. These two passages may be referring to elders, but they don't identify them as such.

Contrary to the episcopal form of government, where the bishop leads from outside the church, the Presbyterian form works through elders who lead from within the church. Thus they are much closer to the church and would likely have a better understanding of the church in general and its financial needs in particular.

The Congregation Has the Power

The congregational form of polity gives power to the congregation to exercise influence over its affairs. Churches that practice this view emphasize that the church is to be a democratic community that vests ultimate authority in the membership or congregation. They acknowledge Christ as head of the church and often elect ministers to lead them who theoretically have no more power than any other member of the congregation. They also elect boards (elder, deacon, and others) to lead and conduct much of the church's business. Baptists and numerous other denominational and independent churches practice this polity.

Is this view biblical? A primary argument for a congregational polity is the priesthood of the believer (1 Peter 2:5, 9). Passages that imply that congregations in the early churches made decisions in certain situations are also used to argue for this form (Acts 6:3, 5; 15:22; 2 Cor. 8:19). Another argument is the congregation's involvement in church discipline (Matt. 18:17; 1 Cor. 5:4–5). These passages seem to indicate that congregations were responsible for making decisions.

This form of polity seems better than the episcopal form because the congregation, which is the church, is closer to what is taking place in the church. However, it's unlikely that an entire congregation would have the time to devote to studying issues and contemplating data and be as familiar with the general affairs of the church and its finances in particular as a select group of elders who see such a process as their primary ministry. It's also doubtful that an entire congregation made up of both young and older Christians—with or without the gifts of discernment and leadership—could make wise decisions as consistently as a group of Spirit-led mature believers uniquely gifted for the task.

Others Who May Have the Power

In addition to bishops, elders, and the congregation, there are others in the church who may have power. One example is the senior pastor of a church. If this person planted the church or if he's a very strong personality, he may find that when he speaks, everyone listens. We call these "pastor-led churches," and there seems to be some biblical warrant for this approach as found in 1 Thessalonians 5:12–13 and Hebrews 13:17.

In these pastor-led churches, congregations and boards look to their pastor for leadership and help in the decision-making process in general and about finances in particular. And this may be good or bad, depending on his character and leadership skills. Certainly he would be closer to the church, understand its needs, and, if he has financial expertise, should be able to address its finances with wisdom. A particular problem that often arises in pastor-led situations, however, is accountability. If the pastor has all the power, who holds him accountable?

In some churches various committees have the power. When we use the term *committee*, we're not referring to a central governing board. Instead, we're referring to groups of people who serve on various committees, such as a financial committee, or a benevolence committee. This diffused system of governance may or may not have a unifying group or individual that gives coordination to all the committees. We would refer to these churches as "committee-led churches."

While we believe that it can be helpful for either the governing board or pastor to set up certain committees, they should be established to assist the leaders in some matter. We believe they should have no decision-making power whatsoever. Committees tend to have all authority in making decisions and no responsibility in implementation. Often these people are selected because of expertise (such as a construction professional on the building committee), and they may or may not have spiritual qualifications. We know of no biblical support for the committee-led church.

The church patriarch and/or matriarch may have the power. Often such a person is found in smaller, perhaps more rural churches that make up a large number of the churches sprinkled all across North America and beyond. We refer to these as "patriarch- or matriarch-led churches." These people tend to be older members of the congregation who have been a part of the church since its inception. And over the years, due to their spiritual maturity, longevity, or giving patterns, they have accumulated the respect of the congregation who look to them to make or help make the church's decisions.

Many young seminary graduates with little experience have not understood the power of the patriarch or matriarch in their churches. They think that as pastors they have far more power than they do. However, when some issue comes up, they discover that the people look to the patriarch or matriarch to decide the matter, not them. This is especially true concerning the church's finances. Our advice to young pastors who find themselves in these situations is to cultivate a relationship of cooperation with these people. Regularly meet with them and pray with them. And you would be wise to get their input on any major decisions that go before the congregation.

Some Advice for Pastors

When pastors identify with a particular church or denomination, they accept (or should accept) the organization's existing polity structure. Therefore leaders in general and pastors in particular should consider the polity issue before connecting with a church. Do they agree with how the church handles power, at least on paper or by tradition or denomination? We question the wisdom of pastors who take a church without knowing their polity and the relationship of the pastor with the church's board. We question even more those who take a church but disagree with the polity or board relationship.

Who Should Have the Power?

As we saw above, the congregational and presbyterian forms of polity appear to have the most biblical support. There are specific passages of Scripture that seem to validate either form. However, Charles Ryrie accurately observes: "The New Testament picture seems to include a blend of congregational and federal government, limited to the local level."[1]

Apparently, the early churches embraced various structures within the federal and congregational forms for handling power that conformed best to their unique circumstances. That is likely the reason we see a blending of the two positions. It would appear that churches today are free to choose their polity, as long as it conforms to clear prescriptive passages and doesn't violate Scripture. In short, within certain parameters, Scripture leaves it up to each church to determine its own structures for handling power and authority and, ultimately, its finances. Consequently, each church is free to determine how it will structure itself to deal with power and its potential abuse.

Two Guiding Biblical Principles

In addition to the passages above regarding the federal and congregational views, there are some other biblical principles that can help churches to structure themselves as they attempt to handle their power and make decisions regarding finances.

Obey Your Leaders

One principle that Scripture prescribes is that people obey their leaders. In Hebrews 13:17 the writer says to the people, "Obey your leaders and submit to their authority. . . . Obey them so that their work will be a joy, not a burden, for that would be of no advantage to you." This passage is clear that the leaders in the church, whether elders or others, have authority and that followers are to follow them as leaders within certain parameters.

Pursue the Counsel of Others

Another principle is that it's wise for leaders to pursue the counsel of others. In several places, Proverbs encourages believers to seek the advice of several people, because there is wisdom in gaining the viewpoint of others (Prov. 11:14; 15:22; 20:18; 24:6). The point is that all of us are wiser than one of us. We believe that churches are wise to have good, godly, competent governing boards. We'll say more about this below.

Two Scenarios for Handling Power

The federal and congregational views or a combination have the most biblical support and are practiced by most churches, at least in the West. The following two scenarios showing the distribution of power reveal that the church's polity affects how they handle finances. The advantage of both is that they clearly spell out the lines of authority between the board, the pastor, and the congregation as well as achieve a reasonable balance of power.

The Congregational Scenario

This scenario places much of the power in the hands of the congregation. However, the congregation may exercise that power only as a body, such as when they come together to vote on some issue. The congregation might vote on the board members as well as approve the church's budget. No individual congregant, including the senior pastor and staff, has power over anyone else.

The board has corporate power to act on behalf of the congregation. If the congregation doesn't agree with the board's decisions, it can vote out all or some of the board members at its next official meeting. Regardless, no board member has power over anyone else. (An exception is when he or she is leading a ministry within the church. Then he or she would have some individual authority over those in that ministry—Hebrews 13:17.)

The senior pastor is a board member with one vote that he exercises when the board acts corporately. He also has individual power over board members, staff, and individual congregants as the congregation's recognized leader (Heb. 13:7, 17). Other leaders in the church would have some individual authority over those that minister under them. However, neither the pastor nor other leaders have individual power over the congregation as a whole.

This is our scenario at Lake Pointe, and it has worked well for us. We say we are congregation-ruled (the congregation elects the elders and approves the budget), elder-led (the elder board supervises the pastor on behalf of the congregation), and staff-managed (the pastor supervises the rest of the staff, who are given great freedom to execute their ministries without micromanagement from the board).

The Federal Scenario

The federal scenario places much of the power in the hands of the board. The board, and not the congregation, selects its own members. The idea is that the most spiritual, godly leaders in the church serve on this board. However, they may exercise power only corporately as a board. No board member may exercise power over the senior pastor or staff (they may have individual authority over congregants who are part of a ministry they lead).

The pastor should be on the board but has only one vote (like any other board member) when making corporate decisions, including financial decisions. However, as the senior pastor and leader of the church, he has individual power over individual board members, the staff, and the congregation (Heb. 13:7, 17).

The congregation has no corporate or individual power. While it may have many godly members, it also has those that are uncommitted and/or carnal, and possibly there are some unsaved people who shouldn't be involved in making decisions that affect the spiritual vitality or financial viability of the church.

One Festering Problem

One festering problem, however, is that some pastors don't know how to lead their churches, work with their boards, or handle finances. They take a church, grow impatient with the board, and tend not to stay long enough to win the board's trust to lead. Others are simply gifted Bible preachers or teachers but not leaders with any financial expertise. Still others view the pastoral role as that of a chaplain or one who merely cares for the sheep. Far too many don't really understand the importance of—or the financial side of—the church. Thus well-intentioned lay governing boards or patriarchs or matriarchs find themselves in a leadership vacuum. Sensing the need for leadership, they step up and take control of the church and often of its funds as well.

Consequently lay governing boards lead the majority of churches in America. This doesn't have to be a bad situation if they don't become micromanagers of the ministry. If we're to have better leadership in our churches, however, our lay governing boards must pursue training and improve as leaders in the board context. This training would involve character work; clarifying the lines of authority between the board, the pastor, and the congregation; and in most cases the adoption of a policy governance model. Aubrey addresses this model in his book *Leading Leaders*.[2]

An Application

How does a church's polity work at the grass roots? What are the practical problems that churches with varying views of polity face when addressing finances in their ministries?

Some Problems

One problem we have observed is that far too many churches don't include the staff or lay leaders, who are responsible for carrying out the church's ministry, in making spending decisions for these ministries. For example, in churches with a strict congregational polity (most often small churches), congregations that don't or can't possibly have all the data needed to make funding decisions for its ministries are, nonetheless, making those decisions.

Another problem is evident in the presbyterian or elder-rule type of church where the board makes all the decisions, including the funding of ministries. This can be less troublesome than the congregational approach, because a board can take the time to acquaint itself with all the details of the church's ministries. However, they don't necessarily lead or manage the ministries, so they're not the best people to make detailed decisions about the allocation of finances for them.

In the pastor-led church, where the pastor or staff makes all the funding decisions for its ministries, there can also be problems. This would seem to be a better method than the congregational or elder-led approach, because pastors and staff should know best the needs of their ministries. However, as we saw above, there can be a problem with a lack of accountability.

Perhaps we can grasp this dilemma best by constructing a funding continuum. On the one extreme there are those who make the decisions as to how the church spends its money on its ministries. We'll call them the "spending decision makers." At the other extreme are the people who have to lead the ministries and work with the funds allotted to them by the "spending decision makers." We call them the "ministry decision makers."

Funding Continuum

spending decision makers   ⇨ ---------------------- ⇦   ministry decision makers

Initially, the spending decision makers and the ministry decision makers may be very far apart, which isn't good, because to best allocate funding the spending decision makers need to know well the ministry requirements of the ministry decision makers. Otherwise they exercise undue control over those ministries and may allocate funds that are not needed or could be better spent in other ministries. Therefore, the key to effective funding is to move both groups along the continuum toward one another, because the closer they are, the better they can communicate with each other as both groups seek to implement the mission and functions of the church.

A Solution

Like most Baptist churches, Lake Pointe Church's polity is congregational. Unlike most Baptist churches, however, we have an elder board. Thus we're a hybrid of the above forms of polity, favoring the congregational form, and as described earlier in this chapter, we have adopted what we refer to as a congregation-ruled, elder-led, and staff-managed approach to power and finances that addresses the problems described above and might prove helpful for your church.

In our model the congregation rules by delegating to the board the responsibility for providing accountability and oversight as to how finances are spent. The board, in turn, leads by charging the staff with managing the day-to-day operations of the church and accomplishing the board-approved goals. In this approach, the board has granted to the staff broad parameters as to how they handle finances. The staff and laypeople who are responsible for carrying out the leadership of the ministry have the freedom to make decisions affecting the ministry within those parameters.

This approach has served us well in bringing the spending decision makers in closer contact with the ministry decision makers. This structure also provides the church with several safeguards. First, it keeps the board from micromanaging the medium-to-small financial decisions that the staff can make quickly, efficiently, and intelligently. Second, the congregation has given the board the power it needs to hold the pastor, staff, and laypeople accountable for their spending. Third, it also keeps the congregation that has little information about the day-to-day operations of the church from slowing the process down.

Let's look a little more in depth at how this model works at the congregational, board, and staff levels. The congregation has tasked the board with responsibility for the budget in general and keeping them informed about any major initiatives in particular that will require significant funding. The board decides the broad allocation of funds to each ministry area but not how it will spend those funds. That is left for the staff to decide. This also gives each ministry much-needed flexibility to respond to a changing environment full of opportunities. Each ministry is responsible for documenting expenditures and results.

The congregation has the opportunity to approve the budget as well as any major initiatives each year, such as land purchases, loans, or construction projects. The budget outlines broad categories without necessarily providing a detailed breakdown as to where all of the money will be spent. When leaders have a positive track record, we've found that most people will trust them. Over the years, the pastor and the elder boards have established a history of trust that has served our church well, especially in the area of finances. After the congregation approves the budget, the board doesn't have the authority to dictate specific spending unless the congregation has authorized it to oversee a particular fund or ministry.

In large churches, the board might choose to delegate its role of financial oversight to a selected group of individuals, perhaps an auditing or finance committee. The auditing committee's job then is to assist the board by making sure each ministry area is spending money as they planned and isn't exceeding their budget. However, as stated above, the committee has no power over the staff.

Questions for Reflection, Discussion, and Application

1. Of the various ways churches have handled power, which makes the most sense? Which seems most biblical?
2. What is your church's polity? What are its strengths and weaknesses? How has this affected the church's finances?
3. Does your church have a matriarch or patriarch? If so, who are they? Has this been a good or bad situation? Why? How has this impacted your finances?
4. Does your church give power to committees? Why or why not? If so, has this been a good or a bad practice? If it has proved to be a bad situation, what will you do about it? Has this affected finances? If so, how?
5. How much power does your senior pastor have? Has this been good or bad? Why? Has this affected finances? If so, how?
6. Do those in power know how to lead the church well, and do they have a good knowledge of church finances? How do you know?
7. Do those in your church who have responsibility for ministries have a say in how money is spent for those ministries? If not, why not?
8. Would Lake Pointe Church's congregation-ruled, elder-led, and staff-managed approach to power and finances work for you? If not, why not?

$\wp\!\!\!\!\wp 7 \wp\!\!\!\!\wp$

Protecting the Church's Financial Integrity

Instituting Checks and Balances

The first involvement I (Aubrey) had in pastoral ministry was planting a church in Miami, Florida. I was young and very naive when it came to the business side of the church. And I recall now with terror how we handled the collection, counting, and deposit of the church's offering. It was very simple. I did it all by myself! However, someone much wiser than I discovered this and warned me that I was not protecting the integrity of the church and I was putting the church and myself at extreme risk.

What does the Bible say about financial integrity, and what can we do to protect the church's integrity in handling its finances? In this chapter we'll present two biblical observations for financial integrity, followed by several practical suggestions for protecting the church's financial integrity.

The Biblical Observations of Financial Integrity

Paul provides us with two straightforward biblical observations for financial integrity in 1 Corinthians 16:3–4 and 2 Corinthians 8:18–21.

Leaders and Handling Church Finances

The first observation is that *leaders should avoid direct involvement in handling church finances.* In 1 Corinthians 16:1–4 Paul guides the flow of the section away from doctrinal issues and focuses on the Corinthian church's practical ministry and care for the needy, particularly those back in Jerusalem. The church heard that a collection was being taken for these saints, and they wanted to get involved. This leads to Paul's instructions on how to collect and send the money to Jerusalem in verses 1–4.

We find that Paul addresses the issue of integrity in verses 3 and 4. He asks the Corinthian church to select several men to carry the collection to the church in Jerusalem, and he adds that if he needs to accompany the gift to Jerusalem, he will go with them. We discover that Paul's position on handling church finances was to be scrupulously aboveboard. Others would handle the money, not Paul. He wanted to avoid any direct involvement with these funds.

With the same desire to handle the church's finances with integrity, the leadership at Lake Pointe (elders and staff) make it a point not to be involved directly in the handling of money. We ask others to serve in this role at the church. We'll say more about this below.

Leaders' Involvement in Financial Matters

In 2 Corinthians 8 and 9 Paul goes into detail about our giving. He says as much here as any other place in Scripture. We know that in 1 Corinthians 16 the Corinthians wanted to get involved in the gift to the Jerusalem Church, and Paul provided them with instructions on how to accomplish this in verses 2–3. However, for some reason the Corinthians didn't follow through, so Paul asked Titus to investigate their situation (2 Cor. 8:6). Apparently he did so, and later we learn that Titus will be involved in the delivery of the collection along with Paul and another unnamed person (vv.18–21). We should note that Paul advised that several people be around and involved in the handling of funds. Should something happen to those funds, others would be present to protect Paul's reputation.

If the leadership at Lake Pointe ever find ourselves directly involved with handling finances, we take safeguards to make sure that others are around to preserve our financial integrity. So our second observation is: *When leaders are involved in financial matters, make sure others are present.*

The Practices of Financial Integrity

In most growing churches a direct relationship exists between a congregation's trust in the leadership and their increased giving. Not only will people follow leaders they trust, but they will give to ministries led by leaders they trust. A major way to increase that trust is to have a good system of checks and balances in place that protects the church's financial integrity. This includes the handling and auditing of funds and a clear description of the pastor's role in these activities.

Handling Funds

It's imperative that every church implement a clear system of financial accountability that governs its financial operations from the time a trusting congregant places money in the offering plate to the time the church writes a check to a vendor. The church must protect itself from any hint of impropriety. Though there is no system available that will keep those who want to steal from doing so, a good system for handling the church's funds can lessen the temptation to embezzle funds or misspend money. We recommend the following four practices.

Use a Group to Collect Funds

The first area your system must address is the collection of funds. One simple rule is that no one should be left alone with any contribution at any time. This is Paul's first observation above. If you pass and collect offering plates in a service, you should charge more than one person with the responsibility of carrying them to some central area and placing them in one container.

Then a group of people should carry that container to a secure safe. These people should not be in the same family and whenever possible should include at least one staff member and one layperson. In a large church you may also want to employ the services of a police or security officer. At Lake Pointe we have a policeman visually present at our central receiving area where we gather the various offering plates.

When the carriers arrive in the secure location, they place the money in a bag that has a lock on it, and then drop it into a roll safe (a safe into which you make deposits but no one person can open). If you don't have such a bag or safe, it's imperative that you purchase one for the protection of your people and system.

Should you have several services, various ushers or carriers for each service can make multiple deposits in the same safe. However, they will not have access to previous deposits made on that same day. The people dropping deposits into the safe should not have keys to it.

Be sure never to leave money overnight in a file cabinet or drawer or any area where someone has individual access to it. If you have any other church entities that generate revenue, such as a café, bookstore, event sign-ups, and other collections, those responsible should follow the same procedures and use the same safe. (Label separate deposits accordingly to avoid confusion.)

Use a Group to Count Funds

There should also be a procedure in place for counting the funds. It begins with removing the collection from the church's safe. Once again one person should never do this alone. Two or more people will open the safe and one may have responsibility for the key to the safe while another has responsibility for an additional required combination. Another option is a safe that is opened with two separate keys.

After they have opened the safe, the same two people will take the funds to a designated place to be counted. During the counting, several people must be present and in plain sight of all. At no time should the counting team have their backs turned to each other while counting money. Also, for additional security purposes, if possible a security camera should be installed in the counting room. It protects the counters and provides a tape of what took place in case there should be any issue later on.

At least two people will count the funds with others watching them. The two will compare counts to make sure they agree on the amount of money collected. And they will both sign a form indicating the agreed on amount. Finally, they'll place the money in a lock bag and place it in a safe until it is removed and taken to the bank for deposit. These measures may seem extreme but are well worth the effort when you consider what is at stake. You are not only protecting the church's resources but also preserving the confidence of those who have entrusted funds to your care.

Use Two People to Deposit Funds

The church will task two or more people with the responsibility of taking the funds to the bank. It could also hire a policeman or security person to accompany them. After the money has been deposited, the bank will provide them with a statement of receipt for those funds that agrees with their statement of deposit. The team will, in turn, give both the bank's receipt and their bank statement to the appropriate financial person at the church.

Follow Policies for Disbursing Funds

Here are seven policies a church should follow in disbursing funds:

1. No one should ever write a check to himself or herself.
2. Limit the amount available for a check that requires only one signature. For example, no one can write a check for more than five hundred dollars without a second signature.
3. No staff or layperson should be able to request a check to himself or herself without a second signature, usually from a supervisor.
4. An auditing committee should review all written checks on a monthly basis.
5. The financial officer should submit a financial report that reflects how much has been spent in every major budget area and how that corresponds to the annual budget in terms of the percentage of the budget spent to date.
6. Spend only monies that have been approved in the annual budget. An exception is funds approved by a designated board, group, or individual authorized by the church to make such a call. And this should be someone other than the one making the check request.
7. Require receipts for all reimbursements.

There are other checks and balances that your church may need. Review your system of checks and balances at least once a year to make sure that everyone is following the system and the safeguards are sufficient to meet the current needs of the organization.

Auditing Funds

The church should ask a certified accountant or some other qualified person to conduct an annual audit. This should be someone who is not a member of the church and not involved in the collection, distribution, or auditing of church resources at any other time during the year. A large church may want to consider hiring an outside organization, such as a professional auditing group, to take care of this. After the audit, the responsible person should report the results to the governing board and make them available to any church members who request them.

The Senior Pastor's Role

In keeping with the biblical principle to reject "all that has a look of evil about it (1 Thess 5:22, Knox)," it is our strong opinion that the pastor should not have the authority to sign checks or have access to the safe. This is the church's way of protecting the financial integrity of both the pastor and itself.

By establishing a system of strong checks and balances, the financial integrity of the church is protected, and the confidence contributors have is strengthened.

Questions for Reflection, Discussion, and Application

1. As you read through Scripture, what are some biblical observations and principles that apply to the handling of finances in the church?
2. Does your church have a system of checks and balances in place to protect its financial integrity? If so, what is it, and is it a good one? If not, how can you fix it?
3. What practices do the authors recommend that you don't have in place in your ministry? Will you implement any of them? If so, which? If not, why not?
4. Have you or your church ever had a situation arise where the integrity of your financial system was questioned or even violated? If so, what was the situation? How did you or the church handle it? What were the repercussions? What did you or the church do to see that it wouldn't happen again?

ᎬᏎ8ᏟᏋ

Funding New Facilities

The constant, major challenge for any growing church, whether newly planted or established, is providing adequate facilities with which to do ministry. The focus of this chapter is on building a facility or adding to your current buildings. To address this challenge, you must wrestle with at least three critical questions: What can you afford to build? How will you fund it? How will you spend the money you raise?

What Can We Afford?

Most churches begin by asking, "What would we like to build?" or "How much building do we need?" These are interesting questions. The problem is they are the wrong questions. When you establish your own personal budget, you don't ask, "What would I like to spend?" And the church shouldn't begin this way either.

The right question is: "What can we afford?" It's very important that before you begin to work with an architect that you determine the answer to this question. There are three reasons for this:

1. Your answer provides the architect with some limitations or parameters as he or she designs the building.
2. Your answer will keep you from having to redesign the building several times because it keeps coming in over budget.

3. Your answer will also keep you from designing a building, putting it out for bids, and then finding that you can't afford what you would like. This will disappoint your people as well as waste much time and money.

How Will We Pay for It?

In deciding how much building you can afford, first, you need to determine the total amount of money potentially available to fund the project. There are several primary funding sources the church may use.

Capital Campaign

Most churches need to conduct a capital campaign to help raise the necessary finances for a new facility, remodeling an existing one, or the purchase of land. In a normal three-year capital campaign, most churches should be able to raise one to two times their annual income. Thus it's reasonable to expect that a church with a one-million-dollar general budget could raise an additional one to two million dollars in a three-year capital campaign.

General Fund

Most churches that have needs for land and facilities can service a mortgage out of their general fund. For example, a church with a $1-million budget might use 10 percent (we recommend 20 percent) of its general fund for its current mortgage payment. Thus it has $100,000 available to service ongoing debt out of the general fund. In most economies, that would service a debt of $1 million, amortized over a twenty-year period.

The church must determine how much additional mortgage service it can underwrite out of its general fund. The following process will help you answer this question for your church.

The Process

First, the church must take into account any existing mortgage debt that it is currently servicing out of the general fund. In our example, the church has designated 10 percent of its general fund to service current debt of $1 million. To service any additional debt, it has to increase the percentage of the general fund available for debt service. Let's say, for example, over a three-year period the church increases the percentage of the general fund that services debt from 10 percent to 16 percent (see figure 1). To do this, one of two things must take place. The church must cut back or eliminate funding in other areas of the budget, or the church must freeze at current levels or limit the growth of other items in the budget. Then the church would allocate any increases in the total budget to service debt.

Figure 1

Percentage Increase of General Fund to Service New Debt

Year 1: 10 percent to 12 percent
Year 2: 12 percent to 14 percent
Year 3: 14 percent to 16 percent

Using this approach, 10 percent of the general budget continues to service existing debt, but now the church has an additional 6 percent of the general fund available to service new debt. You'll recall that our sample church has a $1-million budget and has designated $100,000 for existing debt. Now it has an additional $60,000 available annually to service new debt. Depending on interest rates, it's possible this new money could service as much as an additional $600,000 in loans. Even more debt service is possible if the total budget has grown in that same time period because, of course, 16 percent of $1.2 million is more than 16 percent of $1 million.

Now let's return to the big picture. Assume that our church with the $1-million budget decides not only to increase the percentage of its general fund to service debt, but also to have a capital campaign over a three-year period. During the campaign, it raises $1.5 million in additional funds. That means the funds available for a new building project would be somewhere around $2.1 million ($1.5 million from the capital campaign plus $600,000 additional debt).

One way to stretch or increase the building budget even further is to leverage a portion of the capital campaign funds to supplement the servicing of a larger, long-term debt. For example, let's assume the same church with a general budget of $1 million raises $1.5 million in a capital campaign. If it has created new capacity in its general budget to service a $600,000 long-term debt, it wouldn't necessarily be limited to borrowing that amount. It might also choose to borrow more up front and then put less down from its capital campaign into the project. It could then hold back some of the capital campaign funds in an escrow account, using it over a three-to-four-year period to supplement payments on its larger long-term debt. This approach would allow the church time to grow its general budget to become large enough to cover the larger loan. After a three-to-four-year period, the church could conduct a second capital campaign to retire any remaining debt, if it is not able to service the debt out of future general funds.

For example, our sample church with a $1-million budget might raise $1.5 million in a capital campaign but use only $1 million as a down payment on the building. It could use the other $500,000 from the capital campaign to make supplemental payments for the next five years on an additional $1-million loan. This allows the church to borrow a total of $1.6 million. They would service $600,000 from $60,000 of their general budget, and the $1 million remaining would be serviced at $100,000 a year from the $500,000 in escrow from the capital campaign. This would give the church $2.6 million for its building budget. We will say much more about capital campaigns in the third section of this book.

Two Problems

In the introduction to this section, we said there are two potential problems that could short-circuit the above process. The greatest problem related to building project funding is that churches haven't designated a large enough percentage of their general fund to deal with the servicing of mortgage debt. In chapter 4 on strategic budgeting, we recommended that you designate about 20 percent for facilities.

The problem is that some churches have paid off their mortgages and diverted those funds to another part of the budget, such as personnel or programming. Even though paying off the mortgage is a good idea, it presents two concerns. The first is missional. When a church eliminates facilities as a line item in its budget and diverts such funds, in effect it's saying that it no longer plans to grow. A church that is growing will almost always need more facilities and land with which to minister to its people. Even a church that no longer plans to grow at a particular site will still have needs for facility funding for new church plants or satellites.

Another concern is budgetary. To service debt to build a new facility, expand or remodel a current facility, or purchase additional land, in the future the church will have to reallocate a substantial percentage of its general fund. That is most difficult, if not impossible, when you've started new programs and hired additional staff members using that portion of the budget formerly designated for servicing a mortgage.

Our advice to churches that don't have any current building debt is always to allocate some money in your general fund that could be available for servicing debt in the future. In the years when you're not servicing debt, place the money in a building-and-land-acquisition fund that could be used as a down payment. Even if a church doesn't place the money in savings each year, it could use the funds for various one-time purchases, such as a vehicle or for paying for major unexpected repairs, or it could be given to missions. The important issue is that retaining such an allocation provides capacity. That's the key—capacity to service a future debt. It's important that the church's budget continue to allocate monies for a building fund, so that in future years, when building is necessary, there will be money already protected in the budget to service the debt.

Other Funding Sources

In addition to monies from a capital campaign and general fund debt-servicing capacity, the church can tap any additional assets. This would include any existing money in a savings account or any property and buildings that the church could sell and put toward the building project. Be careful here, however. Selling land could be a short-term solution that creates a long-term dilemma.

Another source of funding is a loan from a bank. Most banks will allow you to borrow up to three times your annual income over twenty years for a building project. For example, our church with the $1-million budget could borrow up to $3 million for the new project. Be aware, however, that most banks are hesitant to allow you to designate more than one-third of your general fund to service mortgage payments.

At this point in the chapter, you might find yourself feeling anxious over mounting debt. We will deal with the debt issue in chapter 12. However, you must realize two things. First, it's okay for a church to have reasonable debt (defined as no more than three times annual income on appreciating assets) if it wants to grow and reach its community. Second, the mission of the church is to make disciples (Matt. 28:19–20), not pay off debt. We're not saying it's wrong to pay down or pay off debt, but we're concerned that some people in our churches have made debt reduction—instead of the Great Commission—the mission of the church. This is characteristic of how fearful churches think, not how growing churches think. Some antidebt proponents argue that the church shouldn't spend its money on interest payments. This thinking doesn't always take into account the cost of waiting to build that comes as a result of the inflation of construction costs over time. Borrowing on appreciating assets can be as cost effective as paying cash.

Primary Funding Sources

Capital campaign

Additional mortgage capacity

Additional assets

Bank loans

How Will We Spend the Money?

Once you've determined what you can afford and where the funding will come from, the third question is how will you spend the money? The answer is to build a budget that will guide your spending. The total building budget should include both hard costs and soft costs.

Hard Costs

Hard costs include the actual fixed contract price or the construction cost of the building and, if applicable, the purchase price for any land. It should also include other easily forgotten expenses, such as costs for parking and site development. Site development would include dirt work (changes to topography) and utility costs, such as water, sewer, and electrical services.

Often when planning for a building, people ask the wrong question. They ask, "How much will it cost us to build a ten-thousand-square-foot education building?" Someone will give them the correct answer, but not the answer they need. They have to ask the right question to get the answer they need. Besides the cost of the building itself, they need to know the costs associated with utility hookups, concrete, flatwork, lighting, landscaping, parking lots, and land. Often these expenses aren't included in the hard costs, but they should be. There may also be increased costs for connecting a new building to an existing building or bringing an older building up to the new building codes. If undeveloped land is involved, the church should have someone estimate its development costs. Some land does not yet have access to nearby utilities, while other parcels need extensive dirt work to be useable.

Soft Costs

The second part of the building budget is soft costs. Soft costs include the following:

1. *Architectural fees.* Typically architectural fees for a church building run anywhere from 5 to 9 percent of the total budget, depending on the market. In addition, architects may charge churches more than they charge commercial enterprises, simply because often they have to work with a church building committee instead of one point person. This makes it more time consuming for them, and they find it harder to please the customer.
2. *Consultant fees.* Most likely the church will need the services of several consultants. For example, if you're building an auditorium,

you would be wise to hire an acoustical consultant. Other possible consultants may be traffic and parking consultants and landscape consultants. Seldom are the costs for using all of these people included in the architect's fee.

3. *Furnishings and fixtures.* What type of furniture will you put in the building you're considering? Even fixed pews are not usually included in the contractor's bid.

4. *Audio and video equipment.* If you're building an auditorium, you could spend millions of dollars on a sound system and a lighting system. Even in a small building, you could spend up to $500,000 for basic sound and video capability.

5. *City permits.* The church will need to pay for various, required city permits and building fees and make sure the buildings meet local code requirements.

6. *Testing.* The church may need to fund various tests, such as soil and environmental tests.

7. *Capital campaign costs.* If you conduct your own capital campaign, you will spend around 2 percent of the total amount that you raise on various costs related to the campaign. This would include mail, printing, meals, and so forth. Should you bring in an outside consultant to conduct the campaign, the cost goes up an additional 2–5 percent.

Who Needs to Know?

Once you've developed your building budget, you will need to communicate this information or a portion thereof to several key people, such as an architect, builder, the bank, a legal counsel, and possibly your Realtor.

The Architect

One key person to inform about your budget is the architect. This may be a person with whom you've worked before. If not, look for someone with a good reputation who knows how churches work. Some architects specialize in church construction, and others have extensive experience designing churches. We suggest that you network with other pastors. Talk with those who have been through a construction project, and ask who they recommend. When you have identified several candidates, interview them and ask for references. Look at other buildings they have designed. Talk to the builders who have worked with them. Did they prepare good documents? Incomplete construction documents cause builders to increase their bids because the scope of the work is not clear.

When choosing an architect, be sure to ask who in the firm is actually going to design your project. In a large firm you may be assigned a less qualified architect or even an intern who has had nothing to do with the builders and references you checked. When looking at examples of a firm's work, ask who specifically designed the projects. You want to know what team will be assigned to your project if you employ the firm. Ask questions about qualifications and experience. Also ask God to give you wisdom in the selection of the architect.

After you have chosen the architect, make sure he or she understands what portion of the budget is available for the actual construction of the facility and what is for other purposes, such as acoustics and video and audio systems.

The Builder

A second key person who needs to know about your budget is the builder. If possible, include the builder early in the planning of the project for at least two reasons—so that he or she can do some value engineering (helping make design choices that are cost-effective, based on actual current construction costs) and to keep you apprised of the estimated cost increases, due to design changes or the changing construction environment associated with the project. If this early involvement isn't possible due to the way you're bidding out the project, then find a consultant to work with you. Perhaps there is a builder in the church who would do some pro bono work, or you may have to hire a builder as a consultant. Either way you need a builder to advise you on the estimated cost throughout the design of the building.

Our experience is that architects are not always good at projecting the cost of a project. Because they are not in the construction business, it is hard for them to keep up with current costs of items such as steel and concrete, and they may not have the feel for the subcontractor markets that a general contractor will have. You don't want to arrive at the end of the process and be surprised by an overextended budget after you put the building out for bids.

The Banker

You banker must also know your budget. While we address your relationship with a banker in the next chapter, we will touch on it briefly here. You would be wise to develop a relationship with a banker long before you decide to begin a building program. You want this person to be aware of your church's situation and potential banking needs. After all, he or she will be a key player should you need any kind of loan to fund the building project. Your banker can advise you as to a realistic amount for a possible loan before you spend time and money on planning for a project that would require too large a loan.

The Lawyer

A fourth person you do not want to leave out of the communication equation is your legal counsel. Many of the transactions that will take place are legal in nature. Long before it is even time to build, you will be drafting and signing agreements. You need to make sure that you're protected legally. If you do not currently have an attorney, you would be wise to begin thinking now about whom you could use and taking steps to get to know him or her.

The Realtor

You may want a Realtor in the communication loop. Obviously you need a Realtor if you are purchasing land and not just remodeling an existing facility. Keep in mind that there are different kinds of Realtors. Most likely you will need a Realtor who deals primarily with commercial properties. In some areas there are Realtors who specialize in church properties. The advantage in working with such a firm is that they know what church properties and facilities are available and the specific needs of a congregation, as well as being aware of zoning that affects churches.

Questions for Reflection, Discussion, and Application

1. Do you agree with the authors that when it comes to building or adding to your facilities, the first question is how much you can afford? If not, what do you believe is the first question?
2. What are the four primary funding sources for facilities? Can you think of any other sources that might help you fund your project? If so, what are they?
3. How well is your church servicing its current mortgage from your general budget? How much additional mortgage service can the church underwrite out of its general fund?
4. Do you have any additional assets available to fund new or additional facilities? If so, what are they? Would you consider encouraging your congregation to give material assets such as cars and boats to the building fund? Why or why not?

5. Do you currently know or have a relationship with an architect? If so, is this the person you would hire, or would you look for another? If you don't know any architects, how would you find one?
6. Do you know or have a relationship with a builder? If so, is this the person you would hire for your project? Are there any builders you could hire as consultants?
7. Do you have a banker? Have you made an effort to get to know this person? If not, why not? What will you do about this?
8. Do you have an attorney? If not, why not? What will you do about this?
9. Do you have a Realtor? If so, does he or she specialize in church properties and facilities? If not, is there such a person in your area?

9

Understanding Good Banking Basics

Churches need to understand the basics of good banking and how a bank might serve Christ's church. Too many pastors know too little about the basics of banking outside of opening and maintaining their own personal banking accounts.

But how would they know? Seminaries provide little, if any, training on church finances for their pastoral graduates. And we don't know of any books written on this topic for pastors. We went to Google to look for books on the simple basics of banking and found nothing. We've seen few articles in the various journals and magazines that purposely address practical areas for pastors and those in ministry. And the ones we've seen simply skim the surface. It's critical that pastors and other church leaders understand the importance of planning for their church's present and future needs and the role lending institutions can play. Thus we want to address this vital area so that pastors can understand the basics of good banking and how God can use such knowledge to advance his kingdom purposes.

Understanding How Banks Work

Some of the following information may seem a little technical, and you may not be familiar with some of the terms. Don't let that bother you. Try to grasp the big picture and not get caught up in too many details. (If you know already how these institutions work, you may want to skip ahead to the next section.)[1]

Four Types of Financial Institutions

There are four major types of depository financial institutions that a church may choose to work with: commercial banks, savings and loan associations, mutual savings banks, and credit unions.

Commercial Banks

Commercial banks are considered the "department store" of financial service organizations. They provide services in at least three areas: loans—consumer, business, and real estate loans, for example; deposits, which pay some kind of return because the bank uses the deposited money to make money; and other ancillary services, such as providing safe deposit boxes and selling traveler's checks. Most churches work more with commercial banks than with any of the other institutions.

Savings and Loan Associations

The second type of depository financial institution is savings and loan associations. Technically they are not considered banks. As their name implies, they focus on handling consumer savings deposits and making mortgage loans.

Mutual Savings Banks

Mutual savings banks are very much like savings and loan associations. They make mortgage loans and accept consumer savings deposits. However, they are different in two ways: location and ownership. Most are located in the Northeast, and their depositors, not shareholders, own them. This is the reason the term *mutual* is used.

Credit Unions

There are more credit unions than any other banking institution, but they are smaller institutions and serve members who have something in common. An example is the Teachers Credit Union to which I (Aubrey) belong as a teacher at Dallas Seminary. Like the above depository institutions, they accept an individual's deposits and make small consumer loans.

Three Types of Commercial Banks

As we said above, most churches work with commercial banks, and there are three types of commercial banks from which a church may choose: a commercial bank owned by a multibank holding company, an independent community bank, or a branch of a large bank.

Multibank Holding Company

A multibank holding company (MBHC) is an organization that owns more than one bank. When it comes to commercial banks, MBHCs are sometimes referred to as the "big boys on the banking block." Many are quite large and, while you will likely have one in your area, most are based and draw their personnel and capital from outside the local area. The advantage of using an MBHC is the expertise of the large organization. In a small community, local banks may be unsophisticated in terms of church lending. There are some disadvantages of using an MBHC as well. For example, because it's based outside the area, it may not understand the needs of the community nor its churches when considering requests for a loan. Because it's larger, it responds more slowly to local requests and may fail to offer competitive rates. Ask your banker if his or her institution is an MBHC.

Community Bank

Unlike the MBHC, a community bank is based in the church's area and draws its personnel and capital from within that area. This can be an advantage to the church because it means that community banks are in touch with the needs of the community. When building a relationship, the pastor is working with a loan officer who likely knows about his church and has a higher level of authority and influence on a church loan than an officer in an MBHC. A community bank may also offer a more competitive rate than an MBHC. We advise you to build a relationship and work with a community bank rather than an MBHC when possible.

Branch Bank

Branch banks are simply extensions of either an MBHC or a large community bank. However, they may offer only basic payment and deposit services. They could benefit a church by providing a place closer to the church for depositing funds.

The Organization of Commercial Banks

Most banking organizations consist of two major departments: lending and operations. Banks stay in business by lending out the funds of their depositors. Thus they employ a lending staff with expertise in locating and evaluating potential loan customers, such as churches. Small banks may have one lending officer, or the bank president may act as the lending officer. Large banks will have several lending officers working under a senior lending officer. You can further break the lending department down into business and personal lenders. The church is a business or commercial borrower and will work mostly with lending officers in the business area. As the pastor builds a relationship with the lender, however, the latter would be able to help him with small personal loans as well.

The operations department of a bank handles all the bank's operations other than lending, including the provision of the bank's administrative support staff needed to comply with internal accounting and regulatory requirements. New accounts personnel, tellers, and customer service representatives are part of the operations department.

Choosing a Bank

Now that you have a better understanding of the world of banking, let's address how to choose a bank. Many churches choose a bank because of its location; it's nearby. In other words, it's convenient to drop off deposits. But it is a mistake to make location the only criterion in determining a banking relationship. There are several other important criteria that you should consider when seeking a bank for your church.

The Church's Needs

When possible, a ministry should choose a bank that's capable of servicing all of its banking needs. These needs fall under three categories—deposit services, lending services, and contribution services.

A bank's deposit services involve its ability to handle the deposits a church makes into its account. For example, if it's a large bank, is there a branch bank in your area that would make your deposits more convenient? Does it have a night depository where funds can be quickly and safely deposited at the church's convenience? Does the bank have a courier service that will pick up your deposit for you? (This is a service that some banks now provide to churches.) Will the bank enforce a church's check-writing policies? For example, Lake Pointe has a policy that any checks written over five hundred dollars must have two signatures. Some banks will tell you up front that they'll agree to this but won't enforce it, especially if on occasion the church violates its own policy.

A church should choose a bank that can service its basic borrowing needs. Here are some questions you should ask:

1. Does the bank make loans to churches? In the past many banks didn't like to make loans to churches for several reasons. For one thing, it was a public relations nightmare to foreclose on a church,

especially in a small community. Also, many church buildings in the past were single-use properties that the bank couldn't easily resell to other commercial interests.

2. Is the bank known in the community as one that likes to work with churches? Inwood Bank in Dallas, Texas, is such a bank. Its president is a strong believer, and the bank has a loan officer whose primary job is making church loans.
3. Is the bank large enough to service the church's borrowing needs? What are its lending limits? Is it willing to partner with another bank or lending institution when the church's needs exceed its limits?
4. Ask the banker if they have worked with churches in the past and what percentage of the loans in their portfolio are church loans. The church must determine if the bank seems eager to work with them.
5. Is the bank locally owned (a community bank) or is it part of a larger chain (an MBHC)? (As a rule, local banks can make decisions quicker and offer more competitive rates than those that are part of a national entity.)
6. How willing is the bank to flex on some of its policies that might adversely affect the church? For instance, if you are borrowing money for a building, is the bank willing to waive a payment performance bond? (This is a bond that the church pays up front to a bonding company. It assures the bank that the project will be completed within budget should the construction company go bankrupt. This bond is nonrefundable.) If the bank agrees to waive the bond, it will save you a considerable amount of money, depending on the size of your building project.

A church should also choose a bank that can service its contribution needs. This involves such matters as whether the bank offers automated clearinghouse (ACH) services to the church's members. This is a somewhat new service that some banks aren't yet able to provide. When a church member desires to give to the church but prefers not to write a check or is out of town for business or on vacation, the ACH service automatically draws funds weekly or monthly from his or her account and deposits them in the church's account. This saves the church much time as well as money and could increase contributions. It's similar to some of the automatic payment features that people are using today to pay their bills, such as a mortgage or car payment.

Another service that some banks are beginning to offer and likely most will embrace in the future is "remote capture." This process uses a small desktop check reader or scanner that deposits checks immediately into the church's account. Similar to the processing of a credit card, the church will run a congregant's check through the equipment, which will then take the money from the congregant's account and credit it to the church's deposit balance. With this service, the church doesn't need to take checks to the bank.

A Bank Officer Who Understands a Church's Needs

A church benefits if it selects a bank that assigns an officer to it who understands how churches operate. A good way to find such a bank is to talk with other savvy pastors in the area who have established long-term relationships with banks. Look specifically for churches that have gone through a building program using the services of the bank.

A Good Reputation

As you consider selecting a bank, you would be wise to ask around about the bank's reputation in the community in general and with churches in particular. If you have already asked other pastors to recommend a bank, begin with these. Mention the name of the bank to some of your leaders, and ask what they know about the institution. Do the same with your people who would typically do business with banks in the area. Google the bank's name and see if anything negative shows up. Finally, ask the bank if it works with other churches in the area. If so, then ask it for some referrals and follow them up.

A Convenient Location

A church should select a bank that is reasonably convenient to its geographical location. This may not be possible. For example, a church may choose to use a bank that is large enough to service its needs and has an officer who understands well how churches operate, even though it is on the other side of town.

However, if convenience of deposit is an issue, a church can have more than one bank. It could choose one bank where it makes its deposits, but regularly write checks from that bank to a secondary bank, out of which it would write all other checks. Churches with $100,000 or more in the bank might be wise to have accounts in multiple banks because of the federally insured deposit limit of $100,000. Although there have been few failures and most often the surviving entity will assume any losses, it's not worth the risk.

Also keep in mind that some banks offer services that will offset any convenience issues. An example mentioned earlier is the ACH service.

Another convenient service is a bank transfer. You could set up an account at one bank where you make your deposit and have them transfer it to another bank where you conduct much of your business. If there is a branch office near your church where you could make your deposit, the location of the main branch wouldn't matter as much. Some banks offer a courier service; they pick up your deposit and take it to the bank. In the future many banks will likely offer churches remote capture. You would be wise to explore all these options with any bank with which you might open an account.

"Shopping" for a Bank

At times you may find the need to "shop" banks. For example, if your church is ready to secure a loan to begin a large building project, such as a renovation or even a new facility, you will want to contact several local banks, provide them with the information they need, and go with the bank that offers you the best rate. This assumes the bank has a good reputation and is willing to work with your church. The obvious advantage of shopping banks is that you will likely get a better rate, especially if the bank knows you are shopping.

Our advice is to shop banks when you're looking for a large loan. If you find a bank that's willing to give you a better rate than your existing bank, then use this as leverage. Approach your current bank and ask if they'll match the other bank's offer. If they refuse, then you'll need to decide whether to go with the new bank for the new loan but stay with the old bank for your existing services or move to the new bank entirely. (To provide you with a special rate, most banks will ask that you move all your accounts to them.) So you should consider whether the better rate is worth changing banks. How much will you really save? Another factor is your history with your current bank. Have they treated you well in the past? If so, then you may want to take this into account before making your decision.

To get a good feel for the market, check with other churches that have secured construction loans and compare their rates with the ones the bank is offering you. It's best, however, not to let the bank know where you're getting your information. Also be sure you are comparing similar situations—size and age of the church, and the size of the loan.

I (Aubrey) discussed this concept with a Christian banker who warned that churches should be very careful as to how they shop banks. This is especially true if they're a small church or anticipating loans under one million dollars. His advice was not to take a "hard sell" approach, because bankers will back off and lose interest in doing business with you. As we explained earlier, banks have been reluctant to make loans to churches in the past and may still be reluctant to make a loan they consider either risky or high maintenance.

How to Choose a Bank

Can it service the church's needs?

Does it have an officer who understands a church's needs?

Does the bank have a good reputation?

Is the bank located conveniently to the church?

When should you "shop" banks?

Developing a Healthy Working Relationship with a Bank

Once it selects a bank, a church should develop an ongoing, healthy working relationship with that bank, primarily with a loan officer. An important part of a church's relationship with the bank will involve loans, and the process is much easier when there is already a working relationship in place. You don't want this to be an adversarial relationship but one of mutual trust.

How would you develop such a relationship? A good place to start is to invite the loan officer to the church property. Take this person on a tour of your facilities and explain the ministry to him or her. Then over lunch or coffee, relate the church's past history and future plans. Be sure to include your mission and vision. Remember, though, too big a vision may scare the bank away from doing business with you, because banks are most comfortable with slow, steady growth. You should provide the loan officer with a synopsis of the church's history, including some financial history, so that this information is already on file if and when you approach the bank for a loan. Remember that in the banking business familiarity breeds trust.

Ask what the bank's requirements are for making a loan. What information would it need? Try to determine the bank's willingness to come up with new and creative ways to structure loans. Try to discern its attitude toward working with churches. Has working with churches been a good or bad experience? What is its attitude toward working with smaller churches? (Many banks consider a small church one that has fewer than five hundred people.)

At least once a year the pastor of the church and whoever is in charge of its finances should visit with a loan officer on his or her turf. Adapt to his or her environment by dressing accordingly. Do they dress casually or wear suits? A banker once said that bankers may subconsciously perceive that a church has its finances in order when the pastor has a polished appearance and demeanor.

The purpose of your visit is to strengthen the relationship, update this person on what is taking place in the church (bankers don't like surprises), and learn from the officer what's going on in the banking industry (new products that may be of value to the church). You might ask if funding is tight, the most current lending rates, and the current prime rate of interest (the interest banks charge their least risky commercial customers and that is set by the market). When a new loan officer is assigned to you (and this will happen), establish a relationship with the next officer.

Securing a Bank Loan

There are two matters that a church should consider when it needs a loan from a bank. First, consider aligning the size of the loan with the bank's lending capacity. Every bank has a lending limit to a single loan that they will not exceed. Inquire about that limit.

The second consideration is the loan request. When a church approaches the bank for a loan, it should have a very thorough package prepared for the loan officer that anticipates all the questions the bank might ask. The requirements of this package may vary from one part of the country to another. It will likely include, but not be limited to, the following:

- appraisal of existing property (by appraiser recognized by the bank)
- a survey of the church property
- the end-of-the-year financial reports for the last five years
- the most recent audit of the church
- a list of all the officers of the church
- an organizational chart that distinguishes lay volunteers from paid staff
- a brief description of how decisions are made
- a description of any past capital campaigns
- plans for any future capital campaigns
- photographs of the property if not included in the appraisal
- a summary of the giving history of the church
- a list of the largest gifts given to the church in the last year (no names are usually required)
- information concerning the requested loan

The information concerning the requested loan is most important and should include at least a page with the following: a statement of how much the church wants to borrow, how it plans to use the loan, how it plans to service the note, the desired terms of the note—such as interest rate and length of the loan—and when the loan is needed.

Ask the loan officer when you can expect a response from the loan committee as to whether the loan has been approved.

Banks' Preference

You should be aware that bankers prefer to work with churches that have a balance of power among their leaders. For example, strong pastor-led churches without accountability scare them. They want their client churches to have boards, such as an elder or deacon board, to provide accountability. And they like to see a distribution of power among the leaders. They view the leadership of these kinds of churches as more cohesive and more likely not to default on a loan.

Prepayment Penalties

Whenever possible, avoid a loan contract that includes a prepayment penalty. This is a means that banks use to keep the church from switching to another bank that might offer the church a more competitive rate on a second or third loan. How does this work? Most banks will require that you put all your property up as collateral on a loan and then repledge it on any subsequent loans. If you've pledged all your property on the first loan, and you are required to pay a large penalty to pay off that loan, in reality you're stuck with that bank, and it doesn't have to be competitive on any future loans. This is a negotiable feature on any loan, just like the interest rate. You can ask the bank to remove this stipulation, and if they choose not to, determine if the other aspects of the loan offset this deficit. You can also negotiate an agreement in which only a part of the note has a prepayment penalty, and you can negotiate the size of the prepayment penalty.

Securing Long-Term Loans

A church doesn't have to use a bank to secure a long-term loan on a mortgage. Another option is a bond company. There are pros and cons to using either one. We provide a chart for comparison at the end of this section.

The Pros and Cons of Using a Bond Company

Typically, a church can lock in at a lower interest rate if it chooses to borrow from a bond company, but the up-front cost may be more. For example, you might be able to borrow $1 million from a bond company for a lower interest rate than a bank would offer, but the bond company may charge around 5 percent of the amount of the loan as a fee for issuing the bonds. One of the reasons for this is they have to find buyers for the bonds. Not only might the up-front cost be more, but the payment schedule may be erratic, so the church pays more some months than in other months. The reason for this is that the company sells a series of bonds that expire at different intervals, each set paying a different interest rate.

In addition, the bond company may ask the church to sell some of the bonds to its own church members. We do not recommend this. Often people have the mistaken belief that if they are buying bonds from the church, somehow they're making a contribution to the church. This isn't the case, because they're getting paid interest for their money, and eventually the initial investment and the interest earned will be paid to them. Someone has to step up and pay off the bonds, and we think it's confusing to church members if they're buying bonds and yet at the same time being asked to pay off the very bonds they are buying.

The Pros and Cons of Using a Bank

Though a church may lock in at a higher interest rate with a bank, the up-front cost is usually less. Some banks may charge an "origination fee" (typically 1 percent) for expenses related to the loan. However, most banks will not charge an up-front fee, especially if you have a good relationship with your banker or if you're borrowing a large amount. For the most part, banks do not like locking in an interest rate for the full life of a loan to a church. They prefer a floating rate, although they may provide "caps" (limits to how high it can go) and "collars" (limits to how low it can go). Many times banks will lock in a rate for a limited time period, say five years, so that a church will know what its payments will be during those years. At the end of the five-year period, there is what they call a "balloon," which means the loan balance is due. In reality this just means the church reborrows the remainder of the note and renegotiates the rate at that time. This may seem strange to a pastor since he is used to getting a home mortgage rate locked in for thirty years. The difference is that a church loan is a commercial loan and is subject to a different set of variables. Some banks are now willing to lock in the interest rate for a longer period, but it is not usually in the church's interest to do so. When banks calculate an interest rate, they must take into account the probability that the rate will change in the future. Because they don't know what the rate will be many years in advance, they must calculate a rate that will cover them regardless of fluctuations. A bank can calculate a more accurate rate for a shorter term. Thus, a series of shorter term rates is usually beneficial to a church.

Banks are becoming more creative in how they structure loans to churches. Sometimes, when a capital campaign is involved, they will actually issue multiple loans. When there's a three-year capital campaign, the bank may give one loan that's tied to the capital campaign, so that it is completely paid off as the capital campaign money comes in. Then they will give a separate loan that is typically a twenty-year amortized loan that's paid out of general funds or subsequent capital campaigns or a combination of the two.

It is recommended that unless the bank requires two separate loans that the church take on one longer-term note when borrowing money. This will allow the church more time to pay the note back in case the campaign isn't as successful as anticipated. With funds from capital campaigns, the church may be able to pay down the principle of the note at a faster pace than the bank requires. One long-term loan will require less monthly liquidity than the long- and short-term combination.

Most banks will ask some reasonable restrictions of the church to ensure that the loan is properly serviced. For example, they may require that the church not take out any additional loans without their approval. They may also require financial statements on a regular basis so they can follow the financial health of the church and address any situations when the church can't service the loan. Most banks don't want to foreclose on a church because of the public relations ramifications in the community. The church should cooperate with a bank's reasonable requirements to protect itself. Two exceptions would be when the bank infringes on the church's ability to do ministry and when it attempts to micromanage the use of other church funds.

A Comparison of Bank and Bond Financing

Criteria	Bank	Bond
minimum amount of loan	no minimum	a minimum
interest rate	typically floating or fixed for only a number of years	typically fixed
down payment required	large down payment	small down payment
up-front fees (% of loan)	low fees	higher fees
payment stream	level over time	higher in early years

Questions for Reflection, Discussion, and Application

1. On a scale of one to ten (one being low and ten high), how would you rate your knowledge of banking? If you're a senior pastor, how has this affected and how will it affect your leadership of the church? What will you do about what you don't know?
2. The authors present four criteria for selecting a bank: it must be able to service the church's needs, it should have an officer who understands a church's needs, it must have a good reputation, and it should be in a convenient location. The authors also realize that unless you're a church planter, you will already be working with a bank (unless the church buries its money in a can in the backyard). How well does your bank meet these four criteria? What will you do if it doesn't meet them well?
3. Have you begun or will you begin to cultivate a relationship with an officer in your bank? Why or why not? What do you believe are some of the advantages of such a relationship?
4. As you look over the list of items that a bank will likely require when you apply for a loan, do you know that your church has this information? Are you aware of where you can get it?
5. Having read our section on securing a long-term loan, do you believe that you would be better off if you secure such a loan from a bond company or a bank? Why?

⁊10⳥

Paying the Staff

A vital component of any church is its leadership staff. We believe that as the church's leadership goes, so goes the church. Our plan in this chapter is to address staff compensation. Scripture is very clear that churches must fairly and adequately compensate their staff (1 Tim. 5:17–18). But what is fair and adequate staff compensation, and how might your church determine staff salaries? Our goal is to provide you with some informative answers to these two questions.

Adequate Staff Compensation

What will you pay your staff? To answer this question, we will address three areas: the budget, the basics, and the staff compensation options.

The Budget for Staff Compensation

In our chapter on strategic budgeting, we advised that you allocate around 50 percent of the general budget for staff salaries and benefits. We noted, however, that this depends on the size of the church. In a small church the figure could be as much as 55 percent of the budget, and in a large church it could be closer to 45 percent. Regardless of the church's size, staff compensation takes a greater allocation than any other item in the budget. This is due to the fact that the church is a volunteer-intensive organization, and that it needs to spend a significant portion of the budget on the leadership to enlist, train, and supervise volunteers. There is no budget that is large enough to hire people to do all the ministry. When you hire staff, with very few exceptions, you are hiring people to lead those who are doing ministry. This is the idea of Ephesians 4:11–13. As the church grows larger, it becomes even more important that you hire leaders of leaders. Staff selection—almost without exception—involves hiring leaders, not just doers, of ministry.

The Basics of Staff Compensation

When we use the term *staff compensation*, we're talking about four items: salary, housing allowance, health insurance, and possible other benefits. This may vary in small churches. In some churches the pastor is the only staff person and could be bi-vocational. In these cases the pastor most often depends on a primary or second job to pay much of the salary and any health insurance. Note that we have included health insurance as part of the staff salary package. This is due to the skyrocketing cost of health care, and the church's need to address its pastor's health and that of his family.

Optional Benefits

The church may also provide other benefits, depending on its size. Some larger churches often provide disability and life insurance, bonuses (such as Christmas bonuses and/or merit bonuses), and a retirement annuity to their senior pastor and in some cases its other staff members.

The church shouldn't consider travel, training and conference expenses, computers, business cell phones, and business meals as staff compensation. These are reimbursables and should be included as part of the overall budget, designated as personnel costs. Some churches also choose to provide a Social Security allowance for ordained staff who consider themselves self-employed for tax purposes. Social Security expense is part of the cost for nonordained staff.

After the church has determined what it can and can't do for its staff, especially in the area of compensation options, it should draft a financial support policies document. You don't want there to be confusion about staff compensation that in turn would affect staff morale. Thus you would be wise to formulate church policies that address the basics and options of staff compensation. You will also need to address some of the details, such as the rate the church will use to reimburse car mileage for ministry, expectations for staff record keeping, what the church considers allowable ministry or business expenses, and so on.

The Basics of Staff Compensation

Salaries

Housing allowance

Health insurance

Additional Benefits

Disability and life insurance

Car allowance

Bonuses

Retirement annuity

Social Security allowance

Some churches choose to give their staff one lump sum and have them pay for their own insurance and retirement. This isn't recommended because many staff members will be tempted to provide inadequate insurance for themselves, will not invest in an annuity, and then will hope the church will help out in a crisis. This isn't fair to the church or their families.

Determining Staff Salaries

To determine the salary for individual staff members, you need to consider salary factors, goals, and increases.

Salary Factors

We believe that a church should consider at least the following six factors in computing staff salaries.

1. The size of the church.
2. The scope of the responsibility of the staff member.
3. What comparable ministries with the same position in the same region of the country in the same size church with the same scope of responsibilities are paying. We will say more about this below.
4. The tenure of staff members with the church. This is only applicable if their length of tenure has added to their value in the

organization. Churches make a mistake when they reward staff simply because they've hung onto a job for a long time.

5. Any prior experience, but only if it contributes to the staff person's ability to get the job done well. Simply because a person has prior experience doesn't mean that it was good experience. You want to reward a staff person only for good experience.

6. Any specialized training that equips the person to accomplish his or her job better than comparable candidates for the same position.

You'll note that a staff person's education is not one of the factors listed above. You should compensate staff on the basis of expertise not just education. Thus we believe you shouldn't pay someone more simply because he or she has a diploma. For example, if two employees are performing the same job and one has a college or seminary degree while the other has no degree—you shouldn't pay the one with the diploma more than the other unless the former is performing at a higher rate or level than the latter. We realize that many people will disagree with this, and it may sound strange coming from two men who have advanced theological degrees. However, we believe that a degree is a means to an end and not an end in itself. The end or purpose of a degree is to provide one with additional knowledge and/or expertise. If a person doesn't have this, or if a person without a degree has more knowledge or expertise, the diploma really should mean little when it comes to compensation.

There are some tools available to help you when comparing the staff at your church with comparable positions in churches of comparable size in the same part of the country. The National Association of Church Business Administrators (www.nacba.net) puts out an annual report, which breaks down salary comparisons by size of church, budget size, and region of the country. It is more difficult to compare large churches (with attendance of more than three thousand), because there are fewer churches in that size category that are willing to share information.

From time to time it's probably a good exercise to do your own survey. If you choose to do so, make sure your comparison churches are similar in size and complexity. Clearly identify the job description of the employees for whom you are seeking to do a salary comparison, and then make sure the other churches providing information are giving you a total package based on the same components. Some of these components are health benefits, retirement annuities, car allowances, convention expense reimbursements, salary, and housing allowance. For a good survey, you will need to compare at least a dozen churches in the same geographical area of the country. Be careful of generic job titles, such as associate pastor or assistant pastor. In one situation an associate pastor could be the second person under the senior pastor on the management team, and in another he could be a college intern.

Salary Goals

There are two goals when setting salaries. The first is to obey Scripture. In 1 Timothy 5:17–18 Paul charges Timothy: "The elders who direct the affairs of the church well are worthy of double honor, especially those whose work is preaching and teaching. For the Scripture says, 'Do not muzzle the ox while it is treading out the grain,' and 'The worker deserves his wages.'"

Paul makes much the same argument in 1 Corinthians 9:7–14, where he argues that he has a right to receive compensation but has put aside that right because of others—likely legalists—who have challenged this right and maligned him over it.

The second goal is to retain good staff. The point here is simple. If you don't take good care of your staff, you could lose them to other ministries. Good staff are not motivated just because of the generous compensation, but they should not have to choose between meaningful ministry and the responsibility to care for themselves and their family. The two passages above make it very clear that staff have a right to expect fair compensation. Using the argument that staff should not be in ministry for the money as an excuse for paying less than fair wages is similar to what Paul's detractors said about him in 1 Corinthians 9:7–14.

Salary Increases

Once you've determined a person's salary, you can change it by periodic increases. Thus raises are an important part of a staff person's salary. The same goals for setting staff salaries apply to staff raises—the goals of obeying God's Word and retaining good staff people. There are several types of raises.

Cost-of-Living Raises

If you're in an environment where inflation is a factor (and who isn't?), you should consider an annual cost-of-living raise for all staff. You cannot pay someone the same amount from year to year in an inflationary environment. To do so would mean reducing the person's salary. For example, if the inflation rate is 2 percent, you should, if at all possible, give all your staff at least a 2 percent raise just to stay even with last year. However, a cost-of-living increase may not be possible under some circumstances, such as when the giving in a church is plateaued or in decline. This could be due to a church split, a significant downturn in the local economy, or even poor staff performance.

Across-the-Board Raises

In addition to cost-of-living increases, some churches give across-the-board merit raises to all their staff persons. Others give them to various categories of employees. We don't recommend this universal approach to salary increases for several reasons. One is that it fails to motivate under-performing staff. Why perform better if you'll be compensated regardless of your performance? Also across-the-board raises may actually cause your top performing staff to be less motivated. While the church may reward them, it loses its meaning because the church also rewards the underperformers. As a result, the underperformers stay around while the performers may feel unappreciated and move on.

Merit Raises

The church should give merit raises based on staff effectiveness. Staff must understand that their raises will become effective when *they* are effective. This could range anywhere on a continuum from above average performance to exceptional performance. The increase could range anywhere from 1 to 5 percent above inflation or even higher, depending on the church's income. Finally, the amount of the merit raise should be tied to something measurable, such as meeting the expectations of each person's ministry description and annual goals.

Promotion and Increase in Responsibility Raise

Often, when staff perform well, the church will want not only to retain them but to promote them to higher positions within the ministry organization. Likely this means that they'll be moving to a higher pay grade and receive more income along with their increased responsibility. A staff person should receive a raise when the scope of his or her responsibilities at the church is increased. The principle we want to follow is more pay for more responsibility.

Competitive Salary Increases

Competitive salary increases are raises the church gives when it discovers that others with comparable positions in churches of comparable size in the same part of the country make more money. In essence, when the church discovers that certain people are underpaid, it wants to bring their salaries up to market value.

What happens when a church discovers that it is overpaying a staff person? The problem is that it's much easier to raise than reduce salaries. Therefore, you don't want to penalize the staff person because you made a mistake. We suggest that you explain the situation and freeze the person's salary or continue to give him or her raises but at a slower rate than usual. Should this person leave someday, you could hire his or her replacement at the lower level.

Allow us to pause in this section to show how these raises work in a church. At Lake Pointe Church we have given a cost-of-living increase as a base raise across the board for all staff members, unless they have not done their job in the past year and/or if they are on probation. In addition to the base raise, we have given an additional merit raise of 1–4 percent based on the effectiveness of the staff member. There are times when we have given a greater raise than that, when, for example, we've increased a staff person's scope of responsibility or we have promoted him or her to a job that is at a higher pay grade. From time to time, we'll give a more substantial raise if after reviewing competitive salaries we find we are significantly underpaying a staff member. Sometimes we discover this when we lose a team member and we have to go out into the open market to find a replacement. In the process of readjusting the salary for a position to match a competitive market, you may have to adjust the other staff salaries that are on pay levels above or equal to that staff position. The reality is it takes time to make these adjustments, and the changes may have to take place over several years.

One-Time Bonuses

Another tool for compensating staff and encouraging them is one-time bonuses. The bonus is another way that the church can show appreciation and affirm the staff person for ministry that honors Christ. A church may use the bonus instead of a substantial pay raise whenever employees have exhibited extra effort in a particular year but their job may not require them to do so the next year. If you move them up to a higher pay level, you are somewhat obligated to pay them at that level even if their performance doesn't stay there. By giving them a bonus, you've rewarded them for their current effort, but you can wait to raise them to a more substantial income after you see that they're able to sustain that effort.

The one-time bonus is not tied to other formulas in the overall pay package, such as annuity benefits (that may be based on a percentage of take-home salary). And giving out one-time bonuses in addition to or in lieu of merit increases, gives continued leverage to supervisors. Once a pay increase is in place, a person may lose his or her motivation to exert the effort that a supervisor would really like to see on a regular basis. But if you reward an employee's efforts annually with a bonus, there's a greater chance the employee will stay motivated.

Financial motivation is only one factor involved in encouraging an employee to do his or her best. If pay is the only factor motivating a church employee, you have a problem. However, employees come to expect their salary and tend to take it for granted. By paying them a salary, the church is really giving them their due. When the church gives them a bonus, it's special and is viewed that way. The person feels special and appreciated, and that is vital to good ministry. Such a gift also helps those who are not good savers and those who may have some outstanding debt.

Three Cautions

We close this chapter with three cautions about bonuses. One is that if they are too predictable, employees begin to expect them and consider them as part of their salary package. There's a sense of entitlement and expectation that negates their intended purpose.

Another caution is legal. Remember that a bonus is taxable income because the IRS views it as salary, so be sure that it is included when declaring the salary you have paid to the individual.

Finally, senior pastors should never be involved in granting themselves a bonus. This is the responsibility of a personnel committee, a finance committee, or a governing board. In situations where these don't exist, the church should have a policy that addresses this issue so the pastor doesn't have to raise it.

Salary Increases

Cost-of-living raises

Across-the-board raises

Merit raises

Promotion and increase in responsibility raises

Competitive salary increases

One-time bonuses

Questions for Reflection, Discussion, and Application

1. What percentage of your general budget is allocated to staff salaries? How does this compare to what the authors recommend? Is your percentage higher or lower? Why?
2. Do your basics of staff compensation agree with the authors' basics? If not, how are yours different? Do you include more or less? Why?

3. Compare your staff salary options with those listed by the authors. Do you have more or fewer options? Why? If you have more, what are the additional ones?
4. Has your church drafted a staff compensation policies statement? If not, why not? Do you believe that it would be wise to do so? Why?
5. Do you agree with the authors' interpretation of 1 Timothy 5:17–18 and 1 Corinthians 9:7–14? Why or why not? How do your staff salaries reflect these two passages? Do you know of any other passages that address the issue of staff compensation? If so, what are they?
6. The authors make a number of suggestions as to how you might increase your staff persons' compensation. Did you find this information helpful? Does your church use any of them? If so, which ones? If not, why not?

❧11❧

Keeping It Legal

Churches, like all other organizations, aren't exempt from the law. Both Paul and Peter exhort Christians to submit to the laws established by their rulers and governing authorities (Rom. 13:1; Titus 3:1; 1 Peter 2:13–14). We would go so far as to argue that the church should set the example when it comes to obeying federal, state, and local laws.

The purpose of this chapter is to raise some of the legal issues related to money and the local church. In particular we will address tax exemption, employee taxes, Social Security, and contract labor. Be aware that laws, by their very nature, change from year to year, so some of the information contained in this book in general and this chapter in particular—though researched extensively prior to going to press—may have changed in the meantime. Our goal is not so much to give the final word on these legal issues as to make you aware of them, while advising you to verify them according to current law.

Federal Income Tax Exemption

By virtue of being a nonprofit religious organization, the church (at least in America) is tax-exempt in most situations.

An Exception

The exception is when the church engages in business practices, such as running a bookstore or a café. While an argument can be made that the church does not have to pay taxes on profits, especially when the proceeds are designated to a missions or benevolence ministry, the church should charge sales taxes on items sold and pay them to the government as required by law.

A Second Exception

Another exception relates to land that is owned by the church but is not currently being used for "religious activities." Local interpretation of law varies from one place to the other, but most taxing districts would levy taxes on the following:

- Land that has been purchased for a future church but does not yet have a building on it.
- Land that once was owned by a church and claimed to be tax-exempt and then sold for someone else's development. (Many times the taxing authority will charge a certain number of years of back taxes if it has been previously exempted for religious purposes before the sale.)
- A certain percentage of church land that is contiguous but not yet developed. (Churches sometimes can get around this by installing sports fields, prayer gardens, or designating it as "overflow grass parking.") Please note that tax exemption on land is not automatic. The church must apply for the exemption with the local tax authorities and must do so by locally set deadlines or lose the exemption until the following year. In most municipalities, after a property has been exempted, the church does not have to reapply annually.

Tax exemption is one of the most valuable assets that a church possesses, saving the church thousands of dollars a year. Therefore, the church would be wise to do everything in its power to preserve this valuable asset. While it's rare that a church loses its exemption, this still remains a possibility. A church can endanger its exempt status in several ways, not limited to but including the following: partisan politics and fraud.

The church is allowed to speak to political issues but is prohibited by law from endorsing a particular candidate or party. It's unfortunate that some churches violate this law. We suspect that some aren't aware that they are doing it. However, ignorance of the law is no excuse.

The church, like any organization, is required to tell the truth related to finances, which includes information on loan applications, reporting the income of employees, and reporting any nonreligious taxable income. Failure to do so can result in the church losing its tax exemption.

Employee Taxes

Although a church in most circumstances is tax-exempt, its employees are not. Ministers and other employees of the church are subject to income tax laws.

The current laws allow the church to designate as a housing allowance part or all of the salary of an ordained or licensed minister who performs ministry duties. The church must declare the designated amount each year, since an employee's housing costs may change. The portion of the minister's salary designated as a housing allowance is not subject to income taxes but is included for purposes of computing his or her self-employment tax liability if the person has not opted out of Social Security.

The minister's housing allowance must be declared in advance of payment by some official church action. This must be done in writing—in the church's budget, in the minutes of a board meeting, or in a resolution. In figuring taxes, the minister must be able to prove any actual expenses, but it is best to overestimate at the time of declaration to cover any unexpected expenses. During the year, if the church or the employee discovers that the designated allowance is inadequate, the church can amend the allowance for the remainder of the year.

The amount excluded from taxes is the lowest of the following amounts:

- the amount designated by the church as a housing allowance
- the actual amount spent for housing expenses
- the fair rental value of the home and furnishings, plus the cost of utilities

Social Security

The church is responsible to pay the government its portion of Social Security taxes for any employees who have not by virtue of their ministerial status declared themselves to be "self-employed" for income tax purposes. In addition to the church's part, the church is also responsible for deducting the employee's portion from his or her wages and sending both the church's and the employee's portions to the government on a regular basis. The IRS provides information about the specific rules related to these payments in their guidelines found in Form 941. Also, a helpful publication is *Circular E Employers Tax Guide*.

Ordained and/or licensed staff who consider themselves "self-employed" for income tax purposes are the exception. In these cases, the individuals are responsible for paying all of their own Social Security taxes quarterly, unless they have opted out of Social Security within three years of ordination and/or licensing. While ordained persons are responsible for their own Social Security tax, some churches choose to pay an allowance as an added benefit to help them with these payments. It is important to note that such an allowance is also considered income and is subject to income tax and Social Security tax. After a certain level, salaries are no longer subject to the full Social Security tax but are still subject to a smaller Medicare tax. The church should check with the government on an annual basis to determine the salary levels subject to Social Security and Medicare taxes.

Contract Labor

The church is not responsible for withholding the employee's portion or for paying the church's portion of Social Security taxes for workers who are considered contract labor, such as guest speakers or musicians. These are people who provide all their own tools to perform their job and work for the church for a limited time or project. In most cases, they are self-employed and pay their own Social Security and income taxes. In some cases they may work for an organization that pays their wages out of the fees that the church pays to the organization. In this case the organization would also take care of the taxes. An example is a cleaning company that uses its own employees to clean the church.

A great resource that addresses these and other issues related to employees and finances is *The Church Guide to Employment Law*.[1] In this and other guides, you will find more detailed information concerning tax responsibilities and to whom the church is responsible to pay overtime (exempt and nonexempt issues, which are too complicated to cover adequately in this book).

Because of changing laws, the church would do well to secure the services of a CPA and tax lawyer each year to review all of the legal procedures related to the church's finances in addition to performing an annual audit. Smaller churches, which perhaps cannot afford such counsel, should look to qualified professionals in the church who could donate their services on a limited basis.

You should be aware that church volunteers—like others who volunteer their time to nonprofit institutions—can also save on taxes. For example, they can take deductions on their federal income tax returns for some of the expenses they incur through their church ministry involvement. They can also deduct certain unreimbursed, out-of-pocket costs, such as auto mileage, parking, travel expenses, uniforms, and telephone expenses. These contributions may all be included on Schedule A of the individual's income tax return (Form 1040). They cannot, however, estimate the value of their time and claim it as a deduction. If you would like to know more about this, consult Publication 526 or a tax professional, or go online at www.irs.gov.

Questions for Reflection, Discussion, and Application

1. The authors take a strong biblical stand that churches must obey the law. How do you feel about this? Do you agree or disagree? Have you or your church ever had a problem obeying the law for any reason? If so, what was the situation, and what happened?
2. What are your feelings toward churches being tax-exempt? Do you have any problems with this? If so, what are they?
3. Do you believe that churches should pay taxes in situations where they operate a bookstore or café? Why or why not? Should a church pay taxes on any of its land that it's not currently using for "religious activities?" Why or why not?
4. Are you aware of any churches that have lost their tax-exempt status? If so, what were the circumstances? Do you feel that the church or the government was wrong in these situations? Why?
5. Does your church designate part or all of the salary of an ordained or licensed minister who performs ministry duties as a housing allowance? If not, why not? Do any ordained or licensed ministers get a housing allowance who don't perform ministry duties? If so, what is the rationale for this?
6. Are there any ministers on the staff who have opted out of paying the Social Security tax? What were their reasons for doing so? Do their reasons align with those for which the government allows them to opt out? What do you think about this practice?

✺12✺

Dealing with Debt

Someone once said that there are two things in life you can be sure of—death and taxes. We would add a third for a growing church—debt. Debt plays a role in everyone's life. And what's true for the individual is true for the church. However, we believe that there's much misinformation out there about churches and their relationship to debt. For example, when Christian leaders seek to lead and manage a ministry, it's rare that they don't run up against resistance to debt. And there are individuals in your church who have a theological problem with the church incurring any debt at all. Therefore, we want to address two issues in this chapter on churches and debt. The first is what the Bible says about debt, and the second is what the church should know about debt.

What the Bible Teaches

Be Careful

It's surprising that the Bible doesn't say a lot about debt, and what it says doesn't imply that debt is an evil to be avoided at all costs. A key passage on debt is Proverbs 22:7: "The rich rule over the poor, and the borrower is servant to the lender." In itself debt is a means to an end, and that end can be good or bad. This Proverbs passage serves as a warning against bad debt. The message is that we need to be careful about

137

borrowing money, because when we incur debt, we become vulnerable to the one who lends us the money. We are giving that person a certain amount of power over us.

No Prohibition of Debt

Nowhere does the Bible prohibit debt. In the Proverbs passage, it warns those who go into debt of the possible consequences, including financial bondage.

If someone in your church says you should never borrow money under any circumstances, whether it facilitates the advancement of the gospel or not, that person is guilty of legalism. Legalism can exert a form of control over the church that in some circumstances prevents it from moving forward with its message. We say this at a time when far too many people, including Christians, have incurred substantial debt that has caused all kinds of financial difficulties and hardship. Nevertheless we must clearly state what the Bible teaches, in spite of the dangers of debt. To do otherwise is to say what God hasn't said, and that's wrong.

What the Church Should Know

Reasonable Debt

We believe that it's permissible for a church to incur what we refer to as reasonable debt. The question that must be answered is, What is reasonable debt? Most advisors would say that reasonable debt is when an organization allocates no more than one-third of its general fund income to debt service. (This is in addition to any capital campaign proceeds that may also be servicing debt.) We believe that reasonable debt must be no more than two or three times the church's annual income. Three times the annual income is pushing the limits and should only be considered where a successful capital campaign provides a strong rate of repayment. A better ratio is two times a church's annual income. These are the general guidelines that most banks use for personal debt, and we believe they are good guidelines for the church as well.

The Church's Mission

One of the mistakes that we see churches make on a fairly regular basis is they make becoming debt-free their mission or their primary purpose. While this sounds like a noble goal, leaders who make it their church's mission eliminate some viable economic options and make becoming debt-free more important than the mission that Christ gave to the church. His mission, according to Matthew 28:19–20, is to make disciples! Again, we think a church should be very conservative in terms of debt but should not put limits on itself that are not found in the Bible.

The Opposition of Some People to Any Debt

Most every church will have well-meaning people who oppose the church's incurring any debt. However, many of these very same people over the years have incurred personal debt. For example, few people can afford to pay cash for a house. Instead, they take out a mortgage that allows them over time to purchase the house. When you point this out to people, most will understand that to insist that their church do what they aren't willing to do is hypocritical.

Often those who are most outspoken against debt are older people who have been through the Depression or other difficult financial times. Many have become financially conservative based on their experience. The problem is they have made up their minds about debt at more of an emotional than an intellectual level. They argue against debt based on how they feel about debt, and because they're convinced they're correct, they want to force their views on the church.

Good Debt versus Bad Debt

Bad debt is when an individual or a church borrows more than it can possibly repay. And most agree that this is wrong. The concept of good debt may give you mental indigestion. Some believe that the adjective *bad* should always precede the term *debt*. How can there be such a thing as *good* debt?

The key is in distinguishing between depreciating and appreciating assets. We recommend that you move cautiously when incurring debt on depreciating assets, which include, for example, a church van or programming. Though churches need to buy vans and other depreciating items, you want to buy some things without incurring debt.

While some assets depreciate in value, others appreciate. Good examples are land and facilities. You may have to borrow money to finance the purchase of land and facilities, but the land will most likely increase in value. Incurring appreciating debt, such as for land, can actually be a good investment for the long term if not the short term. We would even question whether a church could buy too much land. We don't know of any church that has bought additional land and regretted it later, unless some of that land was unusable. The worst that can happen is they sell the excess land at a profit. Most growing churches find that they should have bought more land when they had the opportunity. Again, land is usually a good investment. One caution: do not purchase so much land that you cannot afford the other necessary expenses in developing your church. We are aware of a few church planters who bought so much land to provide for the future that they could not afford to build their first building when they needed it.

Fast-growing churches may be wise to borrow money not only to allow the church to continue to accomplish its mission but to actually save money. For example, many churches, in an effort to avoid incurring debt, have put up their buildings in stages, finishing out each stage as the funds become available. However, this often costs the church considerably more in the long term due to rising (in some cases skyrocketing) construction costs. It also presents the potential for having to work with several different contractors based on availability (rather than one general contractor) and the inconvenience of an erratic construction schedule.

Questions for Reflection, Discussion, and Application

1. Before you read this chapter, what was your opinion of debt? Having read this chapter, has your view changed any? If so, in what way? If not, why not?
2. Do you believe that the authors' view accurately reflects what the Bible teaches about debt? Why or why not? Do they handle Proverbs 22:7 accurately? Do you agree with their definition of legalism? Why or why not?
3. Are there people in your church who believe that the church's mission is to eliminate debt? How will you handle this? Does the authors' treatment of this help you in dealing with it? Why or why not?
4. What did you think of the authors' concept of good and bad debt? Do you agree that there's such a thing as good debt? Why or why not? According to the authors' description, how much of your church's debt is good? How much is bad debt?

Part 3

Conducting a Capital Campaign

We identified the capital campaign in chapter 2 as one of several components that should be an integral part of the leader's strategy of stewardship. We see it as a vital ingredient to helping your people become good stewards of God's resources. In this third section, our plan is to provide you with three chapters that will walk you through the basics of a capital campaign for the first time. Our goal is to equip you to understand how the process works in general, but not necessarily to train you in how to take your church through a campaign for the first time. If you have led a campaign before or have worked closely with a capital campaign consultant, this will be extremely helpful in leading your own campaign. In any case, it will help you better understand the process and secure a good consultant.

ᚎ13ᚊ

Preparing for a Capital Campaign

In this chapter our goal is to provide you with the steps that you should take in preparation for a good, Christ-honoring capital campaign. Before addressing them, however, we want you to be aware of several things. First, it's most important that the church know itself well. This means that, when possible, it should have gone through a good strategic planning process prior to attempting a capital campaign so that it knows its core values, mission, and vision. We highly recommend Aubrey's book *Advanced Strategic Planning*, 2nd edition, as a guide on how to accomplish this.

Second, any process must be personalized and customized for each church, because no two churches are alike. Thus whoever is leading the process needs to know the church well so as to adapt the entire process and its steps to the individual church.

Finally, we recommend that you work through a series of questions prior to beginning the preparation phase and, if possible, take an online analysis. The questions will help you understand and know your church. The analysis serves as a readiness inventory to help you determine whether your church is ready to begin a capital stewardship campaign. We have included a list of questions in appendix B, and Aubrey makes his online analysis available free of charge at www.malphursgroup.com.

Now we're ready to walk you through the eight steps that will prepare you for your capital stewardship campaign. You should know that this preparation phase takes place over two to three months, depending on your church situation.

Step 1: Determine the Purpose for Your Capital Campaign

We define a capital campaign as a churchwide emphasis when the ministry's members and attendees give sacrificially (above and beyond their normal giving) to the church. The results are funding a need of the church as well as helping the people to grow spiritually as they learn to trust God with their finances and the church's finances. If people don't grow closer to the Savior as the result of the process, then the leadership has failed the congregation, or something has gone seriously wrong with the process.

It's important to be specific about the purpose for conducting the campaign. Some valid purposes are to promote missions, purchase property, build facilities, or reduce debt.

Promoting Missions

Some churches pursue the campaign to promote a missions emphasis. After reading chapter 4 on strategic budgeting, you may have decided that you've not budgeted enough for missions in general or you may feel that a campaign would expand your mission outreach. Another possibility is that you want to raise funding for a special one-time missions project or church plant.

Purchasing Property

If yours is a growing ministry, you may need to pursue a campaign to raise money for additional property. This may be property adjacent to your current facility, property that you need to purchase for a relocation of your church, or property you need for a multisite campus that will help you to extend your current ministry to another location. Chapter 11 in *Advanced Strategic Planning* shows how you can determine the best setting for ministry and your facility needs. It will also help you determine if you need to relocate your church.

Building Facilities

Growing churches almost always face the need for additional facilities. The truth is that we have to meet somewhere. While the church isn't a building, most of the time it has to meet in one. Sometimes a church needs new facilities at a new site for an entire relocation of the church; sometimes a church decides to build additional campuses as a part of a multisite strategy. Remodeling or expanding current facilities could also be the reason for a campaign. At Lake Pointe we find that due to our growth, we're constantly raising funds to expand our facilities. During our twenty-six-year history, we have been involved in nine separate construction endeavors and corresponding capital campaigns.

Reducing Debt

A fourth reason for a capital campaign is debt reduction. The church may owe money for a prior land acquisition or for the building or remodeling of its facilities. Or maybe the church hasn't been able to meet budget due to poor budgeting practices or a declining attendance accompanied by a decline in giving.

We believe that it is a mistake to make debt reduction the sole reason to pursue a capital campaign. Few people are inspired to give to pay off something that already exists. Instead, we encourage you to make debt reduction part of a bigger package that includes one or more of the reasons above. For example, you could have a 25–75 percent campaign where the first 25 percent goes to missions and the 75 percent goes to debt reduction.

Some projects are easier to raise money for than others. It tends to be easier to raise funds to purchase the church's first land or first building, children's facilities, youth facilities, or an auditorium. It's more difficult to raise funds for such things as adult education facilities, parking, offices, and reducing debt. If funds are needed for the more difficult projects, combining them in a campaign with items on the other list will help.

Step 2: Decide Who Will Lead the Campaign

After you have identified the reasons you want to pursue the campaign and believe they are good reasons, you'll need to determine who will lead you through the process. This must be the senior pastor. Spirit-led leadership is the hope of the church. Without good leadership, any capital campaign is doomed to failure, because a campaign rises or falls as a result of good leadership. Although a campaign consultant may provide step-by-step guidance and another paid staff or key laymen may execute many of the details delegated to them, the campaign will not succeed without the senior pastor at the helm.

The Senior Pastor

In many cultures, including North America, people look to their senior pastor for leadership. If you choose someone else to lead the campaign, such as an executive or administrative pastor in a medium- or large-sized church or a talented layperson in a small church, people will likely interpret this to mean that the senior pastor isn't supportive or isn't as supportive, because he's not leading the church through the process.

The problem is that in some churches the senior pastor may not be a strong leader and is thus unable to lead a successful campaign. In these situations it may be better for someone with leadership skills to lead alongside the pastor.

The Role of the Campaign Consultant

If the senior pastor of a church has never led a campaign, it would be wise to bring in a campaign consultant to assist and partner with him. A good consultant is well worth the cost.

Several Advantages

We believe there are several advantages in partnering with a good consultant.

- *The senior pastor may not know how to carry out a campaign.* It's likely that he has never led a campaign. A consultant can prepare him for and take him through the process.
- *The pastor may not have the time.* Time is a precious commodity, and few of us can afford to waste it. A consultant will help the pastor use his time most efficiently. Because the consultant has knowledge of the process, he will keep the pastor from chasing all kinds of time-consuming but ineffective activities.
- *The pastor needs a fresh, objective viewpoint.* A consultant can see things a pastor may not see.
- *The pastor needs maximum ministry efficiency.* Because campaign consultants have experience in various environments and have conducted numerous campaigns, they bring a wealth of knowledge about what will work and what will maximize the effort.
- *The pastor will get only one shot at doing a successful campaign.* When he attempts something, such as a campaign, and does it poorly or fails at it, there are always people in the church who remember what happened. If he wants to conduct another campaign, those people will remind him of the past failure and oppose his idea.

Some church members do not see the wisdom of using an outside consultant for campaigns. Their major objection is the expense. Fees charged by outside consultants are equal to between 2 and 5 percent of what will be raised, depending on the size of the church. (A small church will be charged closer to 5 percent, because the consultant must expend nearly the same effort as for a larger church.)

A good consultant will more than earn his or her fee by teaching the church what to do, guiding them through the process, and holding them accountable for all the details. The consultant's knowledge and experience will ensure that the church raises much more than they would have without him or her, allowing the church to raise multiple times more than the fee will cost the church. Because of this, it will actually cost the church *not* to use a consultant. It is important to understand that the church is paying for knowledge as well as effort when they hire a campaign consultant. Even if the pastor has led a campaign in the past, he will not possess the knowledge a consultant has gained through leading multiple campaigns in a variety of circumstances and different size churches.

Selection

The following are some qualifications that you might look for in a consultant:

- good Christian character
- proven competence (a good track record)
- theological alignment with the church

You can get most of this information from the consultant's references. The remaining information can be obtained through an interview.

Cost

What will you pay a consultant? Keep in mind what we said earlier: a good consultant is worth his or her fee. Consultants set their fee based on what they expect the church will raise, not what it actually raises. This fee is usually between 2 and 5 percent of that figure. So, for example, if a church is seeking to raise $1 million in a capital campaign, most consultants would charge around $40,000 (which is 4 percent)—a small price to pay for the additional money raised. The larger the church, the lower the percentage. For example, a consultant may charge only what amounts to 2 percent or $200,000 on a $10–million campaign. Since the preparation for a small church campaign is almost identical to a campaign for a large church, consultants must charge small churches a higher percentage to make it worth their effort. Some of the smaller firms and individual consultants can charge less because of lower overhead and a dependency on word-of-mouth referrals versus an expensive marketing effort.

Terms for paying the consultant vary from person to person and may be negotiated with the church according to its income and the consultant's preference. Some consultants ask for three payments: one at the beginning of the campaign; the second around eight weeks prior to Commitment Day, when the people pledge the amount they will give; and the remaining payment right after Commitment Day. Others may spread out the payments over five to eight weeks and bill the church at the first of the month. Still others may accept monthly payments on an ascending scale. The terms should be worked out in advance.

We think it's important that the church and consultant enter into a contractual arrangement in which the consultant spells out his services and his fee schedule. It's important to understand that the consultant cannot guarantee how much will be raised, nor should he or she attempt to do so. At the most, an experienced consultant can give an educated guess on what might be reasonably expected.

Consultant-Pastor Relationship

A major problem that you hear from many consultants is that the pastor doesn't follow the consultant's lead and advice. It is important that the pastor listen well, follow through on any instructions, communicate freely and openly, keep any surprises to a minimum, and trust the consultant, having confidence in his counsel. Church leaders should know the basics of the campaign before signing a contract, making sure that none of its key elements are distasteful or countercultural to the church or its theological beliefs.

The Capital Campaign Team

In addition to the senior pastor and the consultant, the church must enlist and train additional people to be involved in the leadership of the campaign. Of primary importance is a campaign steering committee or capital campaign team that consists of church leaders with reasonable knowledge of what the Bible says about stewardship and a clear vision for the campaign and project. The expectations for each member of the team are that he or she pray for his or her own participation in the campaign, participate by giving a sacrificial gift and a multiple-year pledge, let others know of his or her enthusiastic support of the campaign, and recruit people to work with him or her in a particular campaign area. The team positions are described below (see appendix C for more detailed descriptions).

- *Team chairperson.* This individual will oversee the process and make sure the other team members are doing their jobs. While this person needs to be a leader who functions well in this position, it would be ideal if he or she is a major donor who sets a good example for the congregation in general and other major donors in particular.

- *Advanced gift or commitment coordinator.* This person will work with the team chairperson to collect and tabulate advance commitments from the staff, steering committee or campaign team, church financial committee (if it has one), the church board, Sunday school or ABF teachers, small-group leaders, and key donors.
- *Children's ministry leader.* This leader will develop and implement a strategy to involve the children in the campaign. It will most likely be the staff or layperson responsible for this ministry area.
- *Graphics and printing coordinator.* This person will be responsible for making sure all printed materials are designed and printed on time.
- *Hospitality coordinator.* This person will be responsible for securing the advance-briefing homes, hiring a caterer, and doing setup and cleanup in these homes.
- *Media coordinator.* This person will be responsible for the production of campaign videos and DVDs needed for advance briefings, home prayer meetings, and Vision Sunday, and for all video and sound needs at campaign events.
- *Phone team leader.* This leader will be responsible for recruiting others who will actually do the phone calling to those invited to the advance briefings or other gatherings.
- *Prayer team leader.* This leader will serve as the point person for keeping prayer central in the campaign, leading the emphasis on prayer throughout the campaign, and making sure prayer meetings are scheduled on the campaign flowchart.
- *Stewardship education leader.* This person will be responsible for making sure all the small groups and/or Sunday school or Bible fellowship leaders are trained in how to teach any stewardship education lessons.
- *Youth ministry leader.* This leader will develop and implement a strategy for how the youth ministry will be involved in the campaign. It will most likely be the youth pastor if the church has one.

Other Leaders

The church staff (or lay leaders in a smaller church) will coordinate the rest of the process. Obviously there needs to be one administrative or managing person who is responsible for seeing that everything takes place when it needs to take place. This also involves communicating with all the different people who are involved either on paid staff or as volunteers on the steering committee. In the larger church this could be an executive or administrative pastor, or a gifted layperson. In a small church this would be the pastor or a gifted layperson. This person could be designated the campaign manager and serve on the team with the pastor.

Some churches find it necessary to hire additional secretarial help for a two-to-three-month period during the campaign to assist with all the mailings, emailings, and tabulation of the commitments and subsequent follow-up.

Step 3: Determine Campaign Expenses

When a church decides to move into a capital stewardship campaign, it must set a budget to cover expenses. As you establish your budget, you will need to include the cost of the consultant as well as other campaign expenses.

As we said above, the cost of the consultant will be between 2 and 5 percent of what the campaign can potentially raise. Don't forget to include the consultant's other expenses, such as airplane tickets and room and board.

Other campaign expenses include such basic items as printing costs, video production, additional secretarial assistance, mail costs, and food for the advance briefings. You may also need to include the cost of models of future facilities, an artist's renderings of the new or remodeled facilities, and so forth.

In addition to the consultant's fee, a campaign will need to spend approximately $20,000 to raise the first $1 million and $10,000 for each additional million. For example, if a church seeks to raise $3 million, it needs to budget about $40,000 for campaign costs ($20,000 for the first $1 million and $10,000 each for the remaining $2 million). A church can use funds in their existing building fund for these expenses, since it will be paid back with the capital campaign proceeds. If there is no existing building fund money, the church can borrow from and repay its general account or get a short-term line of credit from its bank, which can be repaid as campaign funds begin coming in. Another possibility is to get a key donor to underwrite the cost of the campaign, which allows you to let people know, if necessary, that no capital campaign funds were used for fundraising.

Step 4: Select the Time for the Campaign

The timing of your campaign is critical. You must consider when to have your campaign and for how long.

Timing of the Campaign

You can have a campaign whenever you desire. Much depends on your individual situation. However, we recommend that for maximum effectiveness you have it in the fall or spring.

Most leaders like to schedule the preparation phase of the campaign in June and/or July and the execution phase in August through early December (before Christmas). A major reason for this time is that it allows the donor to make a financial contribution in four tax years. They would make the initial gift sometime during September through December and then pledge and give the other gifts over the next three years during the follow-up phase. So the gift would impact four taxable years, which would allow some of your larger givers to receive an immediate tax credit. In addition, it might motivate some to make a larger gift because it spans a four-year time period.

If your situation is such that you prefer or need to wait until spring for your campaign, then you could schedule the preparation phase of the campaign for January and possibly February and the execution phase in March through May. Make sure there are no holidays or key dates that might interfere with the timing of the campaign. Also time it so that the majority of the campaign takes place at a time when you experience your highest attendance.

Length of the Campaign

The length of the pledges can be one, two, or three years. Your consultant should be able to help you determine which is best for your situation.

Most capital pledges span three years in length, and we believe this is the best option for most churches. The reason is that it's much easier for your people to give over a three-year period than a shorter period of time, and they can afford to give more this way. A shorter (one- or two-year) campaign takes just as much effort as a longer one, and the problem is that a shorter campaign may require coming back to the church again soon with another campaign. Because of the amount of effort, attention, and expense required by a well-executed campaign, we do not recommend doing one on an annual basis. However, some churches have done back-to-back three-year campaigns when they find that one campaign will not raise sufficient funds to meet their project needs. If they're acquiring land and building a new facility, the first campaign could focus on land acquisition and the second on financing the facilities. The theme of the first could be something like "Possess the Land" and the theme of the second could be "Build for Tomorrow."

At Lake Pointe, we have been in a fairly consistent growth mode over the last twenty-six years. Thus we've conducted back-to-back three-year capital campaigns during most of the life of our church. We've found that our people respond well to this for several reasons. Every time we do a capital campaign, there are a lot of people who weren't at the church the last time we did a capital campaign. Back-to-back campaigns allow us to capture their building gifts and give them the blessing of participating. Also our people consider it a privilege to be part of a church that is growing so fast that it needs to have one campaign after the other. After people have incorporated sacrificial, above-and-beyond giving into their own personal budgets, it's easier for them to continue giving at the same or higher level. And this is much better than waiting three or four years after the first campaign to start another one and challenge them to reintroduce sacrificial giving into their personal budgets.

While a three-year campaign is usually best, you may prefer a one-year or a two-year campaign for a smaller project. You would be able to raise the necessary funds in a shorter time frame. Sometimes the three-year capital campaign does not provide enough money to complete the project, and you might want to add a one-year campaign as an extension, asking everyone to continue to give at the level they pledged for the first three years. As a general rule, it's not a good idea to have consecutive one-year campaigns or a lot of one- and two-year campaigns.

Step 5: Set the Campaign Vision

When you hear the term *vision*, what comes to mind? Lots of people are using the term in numerous, different ways. In this section we're not referring to the church's vision. The church's vision is a snapshot of the future. It's what you see when you picture the church in your mind three, five, ten years from now. For more on this, see Aubrey's book *Developing a Vision for Ministry in the Twenty-first Century*.[1]

The vision of the campaign, while not the same as the church's overall vision, must be connected to the church's vision. The vision for the campaign is narrower than the church's vision and focuses on the purpose for the campaign, whether it is missions, land acquisition, or a new facility. It is the answer to the question, *What do you see when you think about what it will be like around here when we accomplish the campaign's purpose?*

The Reason for the Campaign Vision

It's not enough to announce, "We're going to raise money and, by the way, here's what we're raising money for." First of all, the people have to be convinced that the purpose for the money is a real need, and they must be convinced of this before you announce the campaign and cast the campaign vision, which takes place in the next phase (the execution phase). There are several reasons why you must cast the vision:

- *The vision helps eliminate a fear of the future.* A capital campaign is a form of change. You're asking people to change the way they're giving so that there can be a change in the church. People don't fear change, but they fear the unknown. So it's the leader's responsibility to make the desired future clear by casting the vision and thus eliminating much of the unknown.
- *The vision paints a picture of the future.* When you cast your campaign vision, you are helping your people see the future and what their sacrificial giving will bring to the church. You want your congregation to see that if they give to the vision, something will exist that would not otherwise. The result could be a new church facility or a youth facility or a new children's building.
- *The vision paints a picture of a better future.* You want your people to understand that accomplishing the vision will result in a much better future than the current situation, whatever that may be. Therefore, the results of the change and sacrifice you're asking from them will be more than worth the effort.

Developing a Campaign Vision

When we say you need to set the campaign vision, we mean that the leader needs to develop the vision. This is in preparation for casting the vision in the execution phase. When you arrive at that phase, you want to have the vision in mind. There are several ways to develop your campaign vision. One way is simply to write down on a pad of paper what you see when you think about your campaign purpose. This is what we refer to as the Lone Ranger approach. Ask yourself, *What will it look like around here when we acquire the land and build our new facility?* Or, *What will it look like when we send more people on the mission field?*

Another way to develop the vision is to involve the key stakeholders—large donors and leaders—in the process. We call this the team approach. You get them together at a retreat location or at the church on a Saturday morning. Make sure they understand the need for the campaign and define for them what a campaign vision is. Break them up into groups of two or three and ask them the above question about vision. Make sure each group appoints one person to write down what they envision. We believe the team approach is the best.

Regardless of the vision you choose, the power of the campaign vision as well as the church's vision is in casting or communicating it to your people. You will be accomplishing this whenever you or others talk about the campaign vision formally from the pulpit or informally in the church hallways during the execution phase.

Step 6: Determine the Campaign Goals

The Financial Goal

A three-year campaign should raise one to two times your annual income over a three-year period. For example, if your income is $1 million, you should be able to raise an additional $1–2 million.

There are going to be some extenuating factors that will influence the size of your financial goal. The state of the economy and the number of wealthy people who will contribute toward the goal are two important factors. The "deep pockets people" in the church—people with some money who are very liquid and have a history of giving large gifts—will skew the potential to the high end and maybe even allow the church to raise as much as 2.5–3 times its annual income.

Because you can't be sure about how much you can raise in a capital campaign, we advise you to have more than one financial goal. Set at least three goals—a conservative bottom goal, a middle goal, and a top goal that will be the higher estimate. We recommend that in a normal situation, when the church feels fairly confident it can raise two times its annual income, the leadership should set the first goal (call it a Victory Goal) at the equivalent of the annual income, the second goal (the Challenge Goal) at one-and-one-half times the annual income, and a third goal (the Miracle Goal) at two times the annual income. For example, the church with an annual budget of $1 million could set the Victory Goal at $1 million, the Challenge Goal at $1.5 million, and the Miracle Goal at $2 million.

Campaign Goals

Victory Goal: equivalent to the annual income

Challenge Goal: 1.5 times annual income

Miracle Goal: 2 times annual income

Some people fear setting the goal too low. It's important, however, to remember that the goal does not determine how much money will be raised. And a goal set too high (such as one based on what is needed) can be discouraging to the church if not reached. Ultimately, this is about managing expectations.

We advise you to link construction phases to the goals, because this motivates people in their giving. For example, the church can determine that if it reaches the Victory Goal of $1 million, it would include the site work and design the new facility in phase one. If it reaches the Challenge Goal of 1.5 million it will construct a portion of the building. If it reaches the Miracle Goal of 2 million, it will construct a larger portion. Finally, anything above the Miracle Goal of $2 million would mean the church would borrow less money to finish the project.

Other Goals

While the goal for the church is the amount of funds you desire to raise, you may wish to set several other goals as well.

Spiritual Growth

The primary purpose of the campaign should be the spiritual growth of your people. However, growth won't happen unless you make it one of the stated goals that you focus on intentionally. You must ask, *Are our people growing spiritually as they practice sacrificial giving?* Increased giving is one of the signs of increased spiritual maturity.

Increased Giving

Another legitimate goal that results from a campaign is increased overall giving. If people are giving sacrificially for the right reasons, it's likely that many will continue to give at the increased level of giving after the campaign is over. They discover that what they thought would be sacrificial giving really wasn't, and some find they had been giving less than what they could give. Many will discover the joy of giving for the first time. This increased giving will allow the church to enhance its ministries and accomplish its vision.

Congregational Involvement

Increased congregational involvement is another important aspect of a campaign. The church should set goals related to the number of people contributing to the campaign, as well as the number involved in the promotion and execution of the campaign itself. Research indicates that when people are involved, they are much more willing to support the church financially, because they get their fingerprints all over it and have ownership. The result is they believe in what they're doing and are willing to back it up with their wallets.

Step 7: Establish a Campaign Flowchart or Calendar

Someone has said, "The devil is in the details." We recommend that a detailed calendar be developed and followed throughout the campaign. A campaign flowchart is a listing in chronological order, week by week and month by month, of the various events of the campaign. We recommend that you enter each event or task that needs to be accomplished—and who is responsible for them—for each month of the campaign. This helps to guarantee that nothing is missed. Unfortunately, overlooking even the slightest detail can set the campaign back. And missing certain events could derail the campaign. (See appendix D for a sample campaign calendar.)

The campaign manager, in consultation with the pastor and consultant (if one is being used), will create both the calendar and flowchart. Any dates or deadlines for making DVDs, printing campaign materials, mailing special newsletters, advance briefings, stewardship education, prayer meetings, the Vision Sunday, Commitment Day, Victory Day, and other events should be included.

Step 8: Set the Campaign Theme

The last step in the preparation process is to set the campaign theme. The campaign theme should be a biblical concept or idea on which you base or focus the campaign. In essence we're "people of the Book," meaning the Bible, so we look to Scripture to guide every aspect of our lives, including our finances and capital campaigns. Choosing an appropriate campaign theme is a great way to make sure that what we're doing is tied closely to the Bible.

The Purpose of a Theme

The primary purpose for setting a theme is to focus the campaign on a biblical idea or concept. This focus serves to unify the campaign, pulling it all together. It also serves to publicize and help with casting the vision for the campaign. Much like a piece of thread in a fabric, you should weave the theme throughout the campaign. People should see it displayed prominently on the worship bulletins, any campaign brochures, and even a banner hung somewhere within the facility. We also challenge you to select an appropriate passage of Scripture to express your theme and be the primary text for a sermon. You could select the theme and then the best passage to support it, or you could select the biblical passage and then select your theme.

Sample Themes

We mentioned earlier that we've done several capital stewardship campaigns at Lake Pointe. The theme of our most recent campaign was "Beyond Our Walls." Steve has tied it to Joshua 3:2–13, 17, where God is using Joshua to prepare Israel to cross over into the Promised Land of Canaan. This event had huge ramifications spiritually and historically in the life of God's people, much as a capital campaign does in the life of a church. Much of the Pentateuch records Israel's wandering around in the wilderness, because their sin of unbelief prevented them from entering the Promised Land. But finally, in Joshua 3, they're poised to enter the land, which means they're about to experience a new day. Steve used this theme as the focus of at least one sermon and referred to it in other sermons and announcements.

When Saddleback Community Church decided to build its first facility, Rick Warren led them in three successive, related campaigns. The first was a three-year campaign with the theme "Possess Our Land." The obvious campaign purpose was to raise money to pay for their land, and it went from 1987 to 1990. The second three-year campaign had the theme "Time to Build." The purpose was to build their new facility, and the campaign lasted from 1995 to 1997. The final campaign was called "Building for Life." Its purpose was to raise money to fund several other major projects, and it lasted from 1997 to 2000.

At Lake Pointe we've used "Touching Tomorrow," "Kids 2000," and "Pier 4:19: A Safe Harbor for the Next Generation." (The 4:19 stands for Matt. 4:19.) Another church has used "Dream Big" or "Dream Big—Think Big." You could tie this to Ephesians 3:20, where Paul lightly slaps the church at Ephesus on the wrist for not thinking and praying big enough.

Here are some themes you might consider using. We have collected them as we've worked with other churches. Remember, the only limit to drafting a great theme is your creativity. You may want to use one of the following themes or tweak one and make it your own.

The Amazing Race
A Bold New Vision

Building a Dream Team
Building Christ's Church
Building Christ's Church Together
Building for Our Future
Building for Tomorrow Today
Building on Christ's Church
Building on Our Mission
Catching Our Vision
Catch the Vision
Dream Big
Dreaming Big
Envisioning Tomorrow Today
For Such a Time as This
A Great Heritage—A Great Future
A Great Past—A Great Future
A Harvest Just Begun
The Missions Challenge
A New Beginning
A New Step for Missions
Our Best Days Are Ahead of Us
Reaching Our Community
Reaching Our Community for Christ
Sharing God's Love with Our Community
Starting New—Starting Fresh
Together We Build
Touching Tomorrow Today

Step 9: Meet with Key Contributors

Next to prayer, one of the most important components of an effective capital campaign is the one-on-one meetings with the church's key contributors. This is when the pastor of the church meets with select donors prior to the beginning of the campaign. The pastor is really the only one who can do this, at least in our North American culture. However, he may bring along another key donor, such as the chairperson of the steering committee or capital campaign team, to some or all of these meetings.

The key contributors consist of those in the church with the spiritual gift of giving (Rom. 12:8)—those whom God has moved to make large contributions in the past and those who have the potential to make significant gifts to this campaign. Someone, such as the pastor's assistant, will set up meetings with them, beginning with the largest potential contributors. Typically these meetings take place at a mealtime—breakfast or lunch. They should, when possible, take place before the campaign is formally announced and launched, usually in the preparation phase. It would be good but not essential to have the donor's spouse present as well.

Purposes for the Meetings

There are at least eight purposes for these donor meetings.

1. The meetings provide a good opportunity for the pastor to express his appreciation to these people for their faithful support of the church. He will have done this at other times in other ways in the past, but here he does it one-on-one.
2. The meetings provide an opportunity to make sure the key contributors are fully engaged in the church. The pastor can find out if they are involved in a Sunday school class or a small group where they have a smaller network or community within the larger church community. The pastor will also want to ensure that the key contributors have found meaningful places of service. Studies have shown that those who are serving somewhere in the church give substantially more money to the Lord than those who are merely spectators.
3. The pastor will want to discern whether the key contributors are aware of all the services available to minister to them and their families.
4. If the pastor hasn't done so already, these one-on-one meetings are a great opportunity to disciple donors as it relates to giving as well as other aspects of living the Christian life.
5. These meetings provide a time to make sure the key contributors understand where the church is going (its mission and vision) and why the church is doing what it's doing (its strategy) to accomplish this direction. Likely this will include presenting the relationship between the campaign project and the direction and strategy of the church. If the contributor has any hesitation or questions about the project, this hesitation will affect his or her giving. Any barriers can be removed during the one-on-one meetings.

6. This is a good time to see if the donors understand the church's direction and strategy in general, beyond the campaign. It is also a time when they may want to make suggestions.
7. During the process, the pastor should get a feel for the person's spiritual condition and relationship with Christ. Unless it is already known, this would be a good time to hear about how he or she

Beyond Our Walls
a Bold New Missions and Development Initiative

Gifts Profile

In order to reach our $8 million goal and fully fund every aspect of our bold new missions and development initiative, it is important that each individual of our church is involved. Every gift will not be the same, but each gift is vital. The following is a projection of the number and kinds of gifts that will be necessary to reach our goal.

Number of Gifts	Amount	Total
One	$250,000	$250,000
One	200,000	200,000
Two	150,000	300,000
Five	100,000	500,000
Ten	75,000	750,000
Fifteen	50,000	750,000
Twenty	25,000	500,000
Fifty	15,000	750,000
One Hundred	10,000	1,000,000
Number Unknown	5,000 or less	3,000,000
GRAND TOTAL		**$8,000,000**

The above amounts represent the total contributions of an individual to "Beyond Our Walls" including a one-time gift given in 2004 and additional gifts pledged over a three-year period – 2005-2007.

lake pointe
church

came to faith. I (Steve) actually had an opportunity to witness to one of our major donors, who later in that year received Christ.

8. Finally, the pastor will use this opportunity to ask the donor to make a large contribution to the future capital campaign. The pastor knows from his or her giving record what past gifts have been, and he would be wise to challenge the donor to give the largest charitable gift he or she has ever given. The pastor shouldn't tell the person how much to give—that's God's job. Simply suggest that he or she ask God about an appropriate gift. If the donor asks what that would be, you could provide an idea of what you need based on the gift profile (see sample on previous page) that you'll create for the campaign.

We understand that it will be difficult for some pastors to ask key donors for special gifts to the campaign, probably because they've not done much of this in their ministry and they don't know how. But this is an important part of their leadership, and they must get over any fear or reluctance to do so. There's really no one else who can do this, and it's essential to the success of the campaign. Also keep in mind that it becomes easier as you boldly step out, present the need, and trust God for the results. You can't make anyone give, and you've done your part when you genuinely and lovingly present the need. The rest is up to God. If it helps, be sure to take a godly key giver along with you, asking this person to assist and pray for you during the presentation.

How to Ask for a Campaign Gift

How do you actually ask people to become involved financially in the campaign? There are three steps.

Step 1

After some general conversation concerning some of the issues already noted, thank the donor for his or her past faithfulness and generosity in supporting God's work through the church (if indeed the person has given in the past). Explain to the donor what the church is seeking to accomplish, when the campaign will begin, and the total that the church hopes to raise. Let the donor know that his or her participation is essential for the success of the campaign. Ask the person to begin praying about his or her participation. Then you might say something like this: "John, I want you to consider giving the largest charitable donation that you have ever given in your lifetime. There is no way that I know what the Lord is going to lead you to give, but

I want to share with you some of the kinds of gifts we are going to have to receive to reach our goal."

Step 2

Next you would make what we sometimes refer to as the "big ask." You will show the donor the gift profile and walk him or her through it. This will give the donor an indication of the size of the gifts you are seeking from significant contributors. Then you might say something like, "John, I don't know where your gift falls on this profile, but will you consider selecting one of the gifts on here and let me know two weeks prior to Commitment Day? The reason I am asking you to do this is we want to announce the total advance gifts already received before Commitment Day as an encouragement to the rest of our people."

Step 3

Hand the key contributor an advance commitment pledge card (similar to the regular commitment card but dated to be returned two weeks prior to the commitment card deadline). Provide the donor with a postage-paid envelope addressed to the pastor.

Disciple Donors Who Have the Gift of Giving

It's important to meet with your key donors as well as other gifted people in the church on a regular basis and not just when you launch a capital campaign. It's a lot easier to ask for their involvement when you have a track record of regularly meeting with them for discipleship and encouragement. If you've discipled them individually, asked for their input, and invested in them and their families regularly, then it makes a huge difference in their willingness to get involved in the stewardship campaign. As we said earlier, based on our experience, we believe a pastor shouldn't hesitate to develop a person with the gift of giving any more than he should hesitate to spend time to develop people with the gift of teaching, leadership, or evangelism.

As we write this book, we at Lake Pointe are one year into a three-year capital campaign. I (Steve) have been regularly meeting with key contributors all year long, as well as with some of our other gifted people. While my sole purpose for meeting with them is not so that I can ask for a large contribution, it is true that when we kick off our next capital campaign two years from now, I will have been meeting with key contributors all along. Thus we will already have established a relationship and I won't be meeting with them just for the purpose of raising money.

The Campaign Preparation Phase

Step 1: Determine the purpose for the campaign

Step 2: Decide who will lead the campaign

Step 3: Determine campaign expenses

Step 4: Select the time for the campaign

Step 5: Set the campaign vision

Step 6: Determine the campaign goals

Step 7: Establish a campaign flowchart

Step 8: Set the campaign theme

Step 9: Meet with Key Contributors

Both of our organizations, The Malphurs Group (www.malphursgroup .com) and Strategic Resources (strategic@lakepointe.org), assist churches in conducting capital campaigns.

Questions for Reflection, Discussion and Application

1. What is the authors' definition of a campaign purpose? Review the various purposes they list for a capital campaign. Can you think of any other purposes? Which would be your purpose(s)? Would one of your purposes be spiritual growth?
2. Who might lead your capital campaign? Why this person? Would you need a campaign consultant? Why or why not? Who would be your campaign or steering committee chairperson? Who would be good choices for the other positions on the team?
3. You will need to establish a budget for the campaign. How much will you spend on the campaign? What expenses have we missed that would affect your situation? Where will you get these funds?
4. Do you prefer a fall or spring campaign? Why? If these times don't work well for your church, what time would be good? What dates do you need to plan around?
5. What is your campaign vision? What do you see when you envision your church accomplishing the campaign's purpose? Will you take responsibility to develop this vision or will you use a team? Why?
6. What is your primary financial goal for the campaign (how much do you hope to raise)? How will you arrive at this figure? Will you have three financial goals as the authors recommend? Why or why not? What other goals will you set for the campaign?

7. Why is it important to have a campaign calendar or flowchart? What are some events that you would include on your chart?

8. Why do we recommend that you have a campaign theme? What would be a good theme for your campaign? Do any themes on our list fit your situation? What biblical passage would fit your theme?

9. If you are the senior pastor, how do you feel about approaching the church's biggest donors and asking them to support the capital stewardship campaign? Why do you think you feel this way? Have you ever done this before? Are you willing to do it? If you struggle with this, what will you do about it?

10. If you are a leader in the church or one of the church's bigger donors, how do you feel about the pastor approaching you and asking for a significant contribution to the church? Why do you feel this way? Have you ever been approached before? What were the circumstances and how did you feel about this?

𝒫14𝒞

Implementing the Capital Campaign

After you have completed the preparation phase for the capital campaign you're ready for the execution phase. Conducting capital stewardship campaigns is both an art and a science. It's an art because it relies on certain intuitive calls on the part of those who lead the church through the process, and it's a science because there are some time-tested, predetermined steps that have been proved to be essential to a successful campaign. This chapter on execution doesn't neglect the art aspect but emphasizes the science— focusing on seven key components or activities that make up the successful campaign: prayer, advance briefings, general stewardship education of the entire congregation, vision casting, a Vision Sunday, a Commitment Day, and a Victory Day.

Prayer

The first component of a successful capital campaign is the important spiritual dimension, represented by prayer. Prayer is the most important part of the entire campaign. It's imperative that the leadership bathe the initial decision to enter into a capital campaign, the project itself, and the follow-up in prayer. If you've not prayed long and hard about the campaign, you would be wise to back off and spend some time in soul-searching prayer to God. Prayer provides the divine empowerment for the campaign. James reminds us: "Elijah was a man just like us.

165

He prayed earnestly that it would not rain, and it did not rain on the land for three and a half years. Again he prayed, and the heavens gave rain, and the earth produced its crops" (James 5:17–18). Throughout the capital campaign there must be carefully planned and structured prayer meetings, prayer reminders, and teaching on prayer as it relates to God's provision.

Raising the Value of Prayer

One way to raise the value of prayer for your congregation is to set aside and devote an entire session and possibly more in your Sunday school or small groups to talk about the role of prayer as it relates to the project and the subsequent capital campaign. Another way is to schedule a prayer meeting for all your Sunday school classes or small groups to pray for the campaign.

A possible format for such a prayer time is to begin with information about the project. Then let everyone in the group have an opportunity to give praise to God for the difference the church has made in his or her life. Next, compile a prayer list and distribute it to the group as a prayer guide for the campaign. Finally, try to plan the session so that at least half of it is spent in prayer. Allow time for everyone who feels comfortable praying publically to do so.

The pastor could make a DVD that could be played in each group. In the DVD he would emphasize the importance of prayer in relation to the campaign and its purpose. This would be more inspirational than informational and would serve to connect the spiritual dimensions of the campaign with what is going to take place potentially in the lives of all the believers as, sacrificially and prayerfully, they consider their part in the campaign. In other words, the pastor will cast a spiritual vision for what God can accomplish in the life of the church through the prayers of the congregation as it launches this project and subsequent capital campaigns.

Whom and What to Pray For

There's so much to pray for, including campaign events and key people. These should be listed in a prayer guide for small groups and Sunday school classes.

You will want to pray for the leadership of the church, including the pastor, any boards, the staff, and those leading in the campaign, such as the steering committee or campaign chairperson. Pray for the architect, builder, and other key people involved in the project. Pray about Commitment Day. You want to encourage everyone to pray for the campaign goals and about each family's participation in the campaign. If, for example, you're raising money for a children's building, you might want to pray for the children's ministry and the children themselves. If you're raising money for an auditorium, you might pray for the worship, evangelism, and teaching that will take place in the new building.

Advance Briefings

The second key component of a capital campaign is advance briefings. These are small gatherings in homes—although they could be held in public settings—to which you invite certain people in the church so they will be the first to hear details about the project and related capital campaign. Timing is important. You will need to schedule these events after you've formally announced the campaign, but before people really have much information about the campaign and its purpose.

Who Should Attend?

In most cases you invite your top givers to these briefings. For example, in a church that has a $1-million budget, you would invite everyone who gave $5,000 or more in the last calendar year or those who in this particular year of the campaign are on pace to give $5,000 or more. Also include the key contributors you have visited with one-on-one. In addition, invite the leaders of your church, including any committee chairpersons, ministry team leaders, church staff, small-group leaders, teachers, and any others who occupy positions of leadership, as well as church patriarchs and matriarchs. A third group to invite are your potential largest givers—people who didn't give $5,000 or more but have the potential to give $8,000 or more a year. Often these are professionals who are active in the church. However, when you look at their giving record, you may be surprised they aren't giving more.

Thus you're inviting three groups: your largest givers, your potential largest givers, and the leadership of your church. When you assemble such a group, you will be challenging them to give the largest gifts in the campaign. (Note: Some churches choose to invite every member to the advance briefings. To facilitate this, they invite the three already-mentioned groups to homes and the remainder in larger groups to larger settings.)

If a church chooses to invite only top-tier givers to the advance briefings, they will want to run a brief ad in their worship guide or newsletter informing the membership that advance briefings will be held and anyone wanting to receive an invitation should contact the church office.

This eliminates the charge that the church left anyone out. There will probably be few people requesting invitations.

How the Advance Briefings Work

The church invites twenty to forty of the above people to one of several events, which typically meet in a home. The size of the gathering is important for two reasons. When there are only twenty to forty people, there is still a feeling of intimacy and an opportunity for interaction between the pastor and attendees. Also this size communicates to the donor the importance of his or her participation in the campaign, because it's evident that there aren't many potential large donors. Again, depending on the size of the church, you might schedule anywhere from four to as many as forty meetings.

Purposes for the Advance Briefings

There are at least five purposes for these briefings.

1. They provide an opportunity for the pastor to meet with people and explain the purpose and rationale for the project—such as land acquisition or a new building. The pastor should answer all the questions of the people attending to make sure the leadership and key givers understand the project purpose and rationale well enough to explain it to others. In this way, when others begin to hear about the campaign and the project, the leaders are well enough informed to answer their questions and address any objections.
2. The briefings give the pastor an opportunity to cast a vision about the size of the gifts that will be necessary in a campaign like this, without discouraging some of the smaller givers in the church. When you begin to talk about gifts of ten thousand dollars to several hundred thousand dollars with the church's rank and file, you could discourage some who can only afford to give smaller gifts.
3. When your key givers and leaders are gathered in a small setting, there is an indescribable dynamic that takes place. Picture yourself sitting in a living room with twenty to thirty people, and the pastor says to you, "You folks are key to this campaign. It's only going to happen if you step up and make it happen!" There comes a real sense of responsibility in that smaller setting with fewer people present. When meeting in an auditorium where several hundred or a thousand are present, however, the same people may think,

Look at all these people. I don't have to step up because somebody else will do it.

4. In the small setting, the pastor is able to give personal attention to those present in terms of challenging them to give. In addition, people feel appreciated because they've been invited to this meeting, and they feel affirmed at this meeting for the role they're playing in the church's advancement.

5. Finally, the briefings are an opportunity for the pastor to explain how the campaign works. The pastor explains that on Commitment Day the people will be asked to make a one-time gift and turn in a pledge card indicating what they will give each year to the building fund—over and above their regular gifts—for the duration of the campaign (usually three years). They will also be asked to indicate what they are planning to do prior to Commitment Day. We'll discuss the role of this advance commitment later in the chapter.

Setting Up an Advance Briefing

For a successful advance briefing, there are several steps you should follow.

1. Begin by making a list of your largest givers, your potential largest givers, and the leadership of the church (unless you are including the entire membership).

2. Based on this list, calculate how many people you will invite to the briefings. For example, you may have a list of 200 individuals who represent 100 family units.

3. Identify homes where the groups can meet and have the hospitality coordinator make the arrangements with the homeowners. Assuming that 80 percent of the people you invite show up, and that the average home can comfortably host 20–25 people, calculate how many homes you will need. For example, if you invite 200 people, about 160 will show up, so you would need approximately 7 homes in which to meet.

4. Pick 7 separate dates for the briefings. They can be as little as one day apart. Then invite people—either by affinity group or by geographical location—to one of the homes on the specified date. Send them a nice invitation saying the pastor and his spouse would like to invite them to a special advance briefing about the new initiative (missions, facilities, land acquisition, children's facility, etc.) the church is about to pursue. Also be sure to include a map to the house, the time for the meeting, and whether

you'll serve hors d'oeuvres or a dessert, which the church will provide.

5. About 7 days after the people have received their invitation, ask the phone team to begin calling them to confirm that they do plan to attend. It's likely that some people can't be present for the briefing specified in their invitation. If this is the case, the phone team member can give them the option of attending a briefing on one of the other 6 nights. If they agree, the phone team will notify the church office, and the church office will, in turn, send them a new invitation with the new location and a map. It's important that churches provide free childcare each night. Otherwise some people will not be able to attend.

The Agenda of an Advance Briefing

The Opening

A typical program for an advance briefing could begin with some kind of dessert or hors d'oeuvres for people as they arrive and spend some time talking together. Also we recommend that, if possible, you provide some kind of display for the people to see, such as the plans, an artist's rendering, or even a model of the facilities you plan to build. Display them in a place where people will see them as they walk around the room in which you are meeting. It will make attendees feel special if this is the first occasion that anyone has seen these displays.

The Presentation

After there has been time for socializing, the pastor makes a presentation in which he explains the purpose for the campaign and makes any other necessary remarks. It would be good if he could include a short, inspirational video presentation that complements or adds further information to his presentation. He would then follow this up with some time for questions and answers.

The Gift Profile

The pastor gives everyone a gift profile, a breakdown of the kinds of gifts that are needed for the capital campaign to be a success. For example, the profile might say the church needs to receive one gift of at least $250,000, two gifts of $100,000, four gifts of $75,000, on down to gifts of $3,000 or less. Again you're trying to help your largest potential givers understand that you're not asking them to write a check for $1,000. Instead, you're asking them to make a one-time gift and a three-year pledge, which together would equal multiple thousands of dollars.

In effect, you're asking them to make a gift of a lifetime. The profile can stretch the people's vision of the potential magnitude of the gift they can give when they see a gift profile that has some six-figure gifts as examples. And yet there are enough examples of smaller gifts so that no one thinks his or her gift doesn't matter.

Testimonies

Key laypersons should give a testimony about their commitment to the project, how the church has changed their life and, although not providing a specific amount, give some kind of indication of the level at which they are going to give. If you are building a youth or children's building, you might also have some of them—or their adult leadership—talk about what this project would do to enhance that ministry.

Advance Commitment Cards

Finally, the pastor should pass out advance commitment cards. He will explain that he is asking that they let him know two weeks prior to Commitment Day what they plan to give and what they will pledge. This will enable the pastor to announce to the congregation on Vision Sunday (one week prior to Commitment Day) that the leadership and others have already pledged a substantial amount of the money to the church. This serves as a strong encouragement for everyone else to follow through on his or her commitment. (In most campaigns, if at least 50 percent of the campaign goal is not reached with advance commitments, the campaign will not reach its goals.)

At the briefing, be sure to walk them through how to fill out both the advance commitment card and the actual commitment card. Then ask them to take home the advance commitment card and a postage-paid envelope so that at least two weeks prior to the campaign, they can drop the card in the mail. Note that even though the advance commitment card and the commitment card ask for the same information, they should be different in color and shape, have two different due dates, and be clearly marked "Advance Commitment" and "Commitment," so it is clear that they are for different purposes.

You should also explain that you still want them to come forward, with the rest of the congregation, on Commitment Day with their actual commitment card, but you want to know in advance what they plan to contribute on Commitment Day. Just prior to Vision Sunday, if you have not yet received a key donor's advance briefing commitment card, you should mail him or her another one and another postage-paid envelope. Email reminders can also be sent the day before the advance commitments are due at the church.

Stewardship Education

Another important component of a capital campaign is stewardship education. It's practically impossible for people to act on what they don't understand. One major reason so many people aren't giving faithfully to the Lord is they don't know what the Bible teaches about stewardship. Ideally you would have addressed the issue of stewardship education long before the campaign begins so that it forms the backdrop for the campaign. As you may recall from chapter 2, we encourage you to develop a stewardship strategy that includes much instruction on biblical stewardship as well as when and how to give. However, if you have just picked up this book and haven't developed a stewardship strategy for your church in the past, it's imperative that you do it now in conjunction with the campaign and regularly following the campaign.

Here are several ways to offer stewardship education:

- We recommend that you distribute written material. A great resource we've used at Lake Pointe is the little book by Randy Alcorn called *The Treasure Principle*. It's a forty-five-minute read and presents a basic theology of stewardship written at a lay level. By the way, this book can also be used as curriculum for your small-group studies related to stewardship education.
- The pastor should preach a series on stewardship. We challenge pastors to develop their own theology of financial stewardship as encouraged in chapter 1. This will serve as a rich source of countless messages on the topic.
- Make biblical stewardship a vital part of the Sunday school and/or the small-group curriculum, as we also suggested in chapter 2. While the pastor obviously needs to preach what the Bible says about financial stewardship, this issue is best handled in a Sunday school or small-group context. The format of a Sunday school or a small group allows for a question-and-answer approach, mutual discussion and interaction, personal testimonies, and some level of personal accountability.

Vision Casting

In the preparation phase in chapter 13, we stated that you need to set or develop the campaign vision. The campaign vision is narrower than your church vision and focuses on the purpose for the campaign, whether it's missions or a new facility or something else. The campaign vision is what you see when you envision the church as it accomplishes the campaign's purpose. We assume that you have that vision, because now is the time to begin casting your vision.

Vision casting—helping people understand and catch the vision—is the process by which the leadership helps the congregation connect the project with their values and theology. Also it helps the congregation visualize what will be different when the project is completed, for example, more space or changed lives.

Sometimes leaders will do a lot of work investigating a capital stewardship campaign and determine that they need to pursue such a campaign to address some need in their ministry. After they come to this conclusion, they believe all they need to do is simply announce the idea to the congregation. Then they don't understand why their people won't buy into the campaign. There is much more to the communication of the vision than a mere mention in a sermon or a line in a letter.

So how should leaders cast the vision? Here are six ways that will get you off to a good start:

1. The most obvious is the sermon. It will possibly serve as the most powerful form of information on and motivation for the campaign. A pastor could approach this in several different ways. He could use several sermons to address what the Bible says about stewardship in general and giving in particular. Possibly a better approach would be to address these issues in sermons prior to the campaign, so that he would need to touch on them only lightly during the campaign. This would free him to talk more about the purpose of the project and connect it with the capital campaign and the mission and vision of the church. The pastor could also emphasize the need for teamwork and sacrifice.

2. Another way to cast the vision is through stewardship testimonies from your people. The testimonies should not give specific numerical amounts related to their gifts. Instead, they could say something such as, "We have decided to give the largest gift we've ever given" or "We have decided to give one month's worth of our salary" or "We have decided to forgo a vacation." The power of these testimonies is that everyone can relate to them. More important, however, are the testimonies that provide spiritual insight into the process people work through in arriving at their gift to the campaign. These testimonies let everyone know they're on board in more than just a casual way.

3. Mail to the congregation a series of correspondence pieces from the pastor that discuss the vision for the campaign.

4. One-on-one vision casting that involves personal communication between the pastor and individual key donors is invaluable.

5. In the past, at the beginning of a campaign, many churches have mailed a single multipage, color brochure explaining the campaign. We have found that it is more effective to send a series of minibrochures or newsletters that repeat the information and reveal additional information as the campaign progresses. People will give more attention to a shorter piece, will be exposed to the information more times, and will receive pieces of information when you are asking them to act on it.

6. There are several methods that target those who are visual learners as well as those who aren't. The vision for the campaign can be presented through a drama, videos, a model, or an artist's rendering of a proposed new building, which should be placed in a central location where everyone can see it. If the campaign involves land acquisition, provide color aerial photos and offer to conduct scheduled "vision tours" of the property.

The best approach is some combination of all these methods that will help people understand and support the campaign when you unveil its details. Again your creativity is essential. It is the only limit to effective methods of vision casting. We challenge you to meet with your staff and others to brainstorm different ways to cast the vision.

Vision Sunday

The fifth component to a successful campaign is Vision Sunday (or Vision Weekend, for those who have both Saturday and Sunday services). This should come a week before Commitment Day. In many churches in the past, there has been some kind of "vision event" that has taken several forms. In some churches the "vision event" has been a banquet. There would be a strong push to get people out to the banquet where the whole church would have a meal together. After the meal the pastor would explain the campaign and ask the people to go home, pray, and then return the following Sunday with their financial commitment in hand.

What many consultants have found, however, is that the people who attend a banquet are those who are already on board anyway. And banquets can be very expensive. Instead, to have the broadest participation possible, we suggest you make the vision event a regular worship service, called Vision Day, Vision Sunday, or Vision Weekend, which takes place the week prior to Commitment Day.

On Vision Sunday the pastor would cast the vision for the campaign as described above and then issue a challenge related to it. Because you have some people who are visual learners, one component of that Vision

Day service might include a video presentation of what the project is and how to be involved in the campaign. There should be testimonies and lots of inspirational music. The advance commitments total should be announced during this service.

Explain to the whole congregation what you are asking them to do and how to fill out their commitment card. Pray together as a congregation, asking God to guide the decision that each person will make over the next seven days that will make the campaign either a success or a failure.

The week following the vision event, the church should mail everyone a commitment card, an offering envelope, and a postage-paid envelope, so if for some reason someone in the church cannot attend on Commitment Day, he or she can mail in a gift and his or her pledge.

Commitment Day

One week after Vision Sunday, the church will have its Commitment Day. By this time the people should have decided how much they can give to the campaign, so the pastor doesn't have to go into a lot of detail about the project. Over the previous weeks most of the people have experienced the one-on-one key donor meetings, the advance briefings, the stewardship education in Sunday school and small groups, the impact of the prayer meetings, and clear, biblical preaching from the pulpit. On Commitment Day the people come with their completed commitment cards (see sample on next page) and turn them in at the appropriate time.

We suggest that several things take place during this service:

- As everyone enters the service, the ushers will provide them with another commitment card and an offering envelope. It's important to give them another commitment card and envelope because many well-intentioned people will forget to bring these two vital items on Commitment Day.
- Early in the service, the pastor will explain that at the close of the service everyone will be given an opportunity to walk to the front of the auditorium to turn in his, her, or their commitment card, indicating their three-year pledge, and offering envelope, containing a one-time gift. An alternative way to collect these is to let everyone know there will be a second offering at the end of the service, when the church will collect all the commitment cards and offering envelopes. There needs to be time provided during the service for the people to fill out their cards, in case they have not already done so.

- On this Sunday the pastor could bring a message from Scripture on the importance of commitment, or he might want to preach on participating in what God is doing. He could define commitment, address the reasons it's important in the lives of God's people, and show the different ways people commit to God. It's imperative that this be an upbeat message, not a guilt-inducing scolding. Very little needs to be said in the message specifically addressing the campaign.
- Finally, the pastor gives the people the opportunity to walk forward and place their gift on the platform or on a table or there is a second offering, after which he closes in a prayer of praise to God.

We have one caution: the pastor must be careful during the commitment service not to manipulate or give any appearance of manipulation. The people should give because they feel that under grace their gift is

COMMITMENT CARD

I/WE will share God's love with others by contributing to the Lake Pointe Building effort. These future gifts will be in addition to my/our regular support of the church.

My enclosed gift today $ _____

In addition to the gift enclosed,
over the next two years
I will endeavor to give $ _____
                                        (Begins 1/1/2006)

TOTAL COMMITMENT $ _____

Beyond Our Walls

My two-year gift will be given as follows: (*Please choose one option*)

☐ $ _____ Weekly
☐ $ _____ Monthly
☐ $ _____ Annually
☐ Other _____

Gifts of real property, i.e., land, stock, vehicles, jewelry may be given by contacting the church financial office.

Name _____
         Please Print
Phone _____

Address _____

City _____ Zip _____

PLEASE RETURN ON OR BEFORE OCTOBER 2, 2005

what God has led them to give. A way to accomplish this is to make a statement such as: "I know that, due to reasons beyond your control, some are not prepared to make your commitment and turn in your offering and pledges today. If that is so, please don't feel embarrassed. Instead, take the commitment card and the envelope home, make the decisions or the arrangements you need to make, and mail them back to us before Victory Sunday so that we can include your pledge in the final count toward the accomplishment of our campaign goal."

Victory Day

The final component to a successful campaign is Victory Day or Victory Sunday. It takes place one or two weeks after Commitment Sunday when the church has had enough time to receive and tabulate the pledges and gifts. Two weeks allows time for late gifts and pledges to arrive and builds anticipation for the final announcement. Your greatest challenge will be keeping the amount given and pledged a secret until it is announced to the congregation. In a fall campaign this will likely be late in December, before people leave for Christmas holidays. (Be sure to time Vision Day, Commitment Day, and Victory Day so that they don't run into Christmas.)

As soon as Commitment Sunday is over, and in preparation for Victory Sunday, the staff or collection team will count all the pledges and gifts. They will also check the computer records to identify members who have not yet made a commitment and send a follow-up letter no later than two days after Commitment Sunday. The letter will explain that the church is still counting the gifts and invite them to send their gifts in so it will be a part of the final count to be announced on Victory Sunday. Once again, the letter would contain a pledge card, an offering envelope, and a postage-paid envelope. The people receiving this follow-up packet will not know that they are the only ones receiving this mailing, and there should not be anything in the letter stating that you know they have not yet participated.

We know that all this seems like overkill. You've sent them the packet before Commitment Day, you handed them a packet as they showed up on Commitment Day, and then you mailed them a packet two days after Commitment Day. Remember that you are focusing on people who have not yet made a pledge or given a gift. And they face many distractions during their week, so they may forget that they need to do this. In addition, you're simply giving them yet another opportunity to be blessed by God and to enjoy the blessing of being a part of something that will make a difference in God's kingdom. Finally, you cannot assume they received the material. The packet could have been lost in the mail or misplaced by a family member, and they may not have been present on Commitment Day.

On Victory Sunday the pastor will, of course, announce the final total and say whether it has exceeded the Victory Goal, the Challenge Goal, or the Miracle Goal. Make the announcement of a reached goal in a dramatic way. One way is to have the amount of the reached goal written on large cards. Each numeral that makes up the number should be on a separate card. Invite the steering committee that has worked so hard during the capital campaign to come up on the stage. Give each one a card and have them turn the cards over in order, from left to right, until the full number is revealed. Be sure a special person turns over the last cue card (perhaps the steering committee chairperson, the pastor of the church, a charter member, a person whom everyone knows has made a great sacrifice for the campaign, one of the youth—if it's for a youth building, or one of the children—if it's for a children's building). Whatever you do, be sure to really make a big deal of whatever is raised so that the church can celebrate its sacrifice. Close the service with a time of worship and celebration of what God has done and his grace and goodness to all.

If the top goal, the Miracle Goal, is not reached, prepare the expectation of the people before revealing the number. After the number is revealed, let the people know that you still believe—as others turn in their late gifts and pledges and as new people join the church in future months—that the top goal is within reach. Perhaps the top goal has not yet been reached because the important goal of a wider participation has not yet been reached.

The Components of the Execution Phase

Prayer

Advance briefings

Stewardship education

Vision casting

Vision Sunday

Commitment Day

Victory Day

Questions for Reflection, Discussion, and Application

1. If you are the pastor, how do you feel about inviting people to the advance briefings? Is this easier than approaching individual donors? Why or why not?

2. As the pastor, how will you handle the church's general stewardship education? What will you do to see that your people have a good knowledge of stewardship in support of the campaign? Have you already addressed biblical stewardship in the past so that it easily forms the backdrop to the campaign? If not, why not?

3. How important is prayer to the church? Is it a core value? What are some of the ways you'll encourage your people to pray for the campaign? Will your tendency be to say more about prayer than actually praying? If so, why? What will you do about this?

4. Are you comfortable with having a Vision Sunday, a Commitment Day, and a Victory Day? Why or why not? How comfortable are you with pursuing people who fail to make any kind of pledge or financial commitment to the campaign? If you're not comfortable, what will you do about your feelings?

15

Following Up the Campaign

The third phase of the capital stewardship campaign is follow-up. The purpose of this phase is to continue to cast both the church's vision and the campaign vision so that people who have committed to be a part of the campaign will follow through and those who have simply been observing will get involved. A well-executed follow-up will allow the church to continue to add to its total pledges and ensure that a high percentage of pledged gifts are actually received. In this section we'll address three vital issues of the follow-up phase: who does the follow-up, whom they follow up, and how they follow up.

Who Does the Follow-Up

Just as in the preparation and execution of the campaign, the pastor must continue to be the key player in the follow-up process. Although he may delegate some of the technical aspects of the campaign, the staff and congregation will receive their cues from the pastor. If the church has used an outside consultant, this person should call or email at least a couple times a year to make sure the church is keeping up with the follow-up plan flowchart. However, after the completion of the Commitment Day, the consultant doesn't usually make any further onsite visits, and the campaign team has no real reason to continue to meet.

This leaves the execution of the follow-up to staff or volunteers led by the pastor or campaign manager.

The People to Follow Up and How to Do It

Those Who Have Made Commitments

It is important to follow up families and individuals who during the execution phase have made a one-time gift and made a pledge to give during the next one, two, or three years of the campaign's follow-up phase. They will likely be members and attenders whom God has touched through the church's ministry.

As part of the follow-up procedure, the church will want to acknowledge with a letter the pledges and the gifts these people have made. This letter should be from the pastor and arrive just prior to the beginning of the time period in which they are to begin fulfilling their pledge. Throughout the next three years or, if it's a shorter campaign, during the remaining period, the contributors should receive a contribution recognition statement that states what the original pledge was and how well they're doing in meeting that pledge. A lot of times people think that they are keeping up with their pledge when they're not, and this is a great way to affirm someone's faithfulness but also to remind others they need to catch up to fulfill their commitment. Some churches choose to give a contribution acknowledgement once a quarter. There are other churches that choose to do it once a year. We believe the once-a-quarter acknowledgement allows people to catch up and not get so far behind that they get frustrated and quit giving to the campaign altogether. The church might schedule special offerings (we recommend no more than once a year) for those who have already pledged to catch up or even complete their pledges early to save the church money on interest payments.

Those Who Are New to the Church

You would be wise to identify and track the giving of those families and individuals who join the church or become regular attenders one or two years after Victory Day. Members are easier to recognize and track than attenders, and it's more difficult to follow up on attenders in a large church than in a small church. However, if you have your people register their attendance at your worship services, including their names and addresses, you probably know who they are and should be able to contact and communicate with them. Do everything possible to encourage them to become a part of the campaign.

Following the initial campaign and even if the campaign is nearly over, give your new members the opportunity to join in the campaign. We advise every church to have a new members orientation or class. In addition to other matters, use this as a time to challenge your new people to become involved in the capital campaign. This could also be done during some type of new member event; the church should contact new church members, tell them about the campaign, and give them a modified campaign pledge card so they can give a one-time gift and then pledge to give during the remaining months of the capital campaign.

Inform regular attenders who are not yet members about the project and give them a way to contribute. An annual letter from the pastor with a postage-paid envelope is one way to give these attenders an opportunity to participate.

If you have not reached the top goal in the original campaign, new members and attenders may help reach that milestone. If you have reached the goal, then challenge them to give toward providing some additional playground equipment, furnishings, or other expansion that will serve as additional motivation for those new members' and attenders' gifts. No one gets very excited about giving to a campaign that has already reached all of its goals, the results of which will essentially be the same whether or not they give.

Those Who Have Not Made a Commitment

In every church and in every campaign, there will be those—both members and attenders—who don't respond during the execution phase of the campaign. Perhaps they planned to give but are procrastinators. Or their plan to give was interrupted by some pressing event, such as a death of a loved one or temporary financial pressures. Some don't plan to give because they don't believe they can afford to do so. These are people who don't understand biblical stewardship and aren't familiar with proportional giving. There are always some people who refuse to give because they disagree with the capital campaign approach to fund-raising.

Regardless of the reason these people don't give, you should continue to gently pursue them. It's likely that with some continued pursuit and God's never-ending work in their lives, some will eventually give. We believe that if you address some of these issues over time and continue to give opportunities for participation without any high-pressure tactics, some will realize that they should give.

You could follow them up with the methods described above. You could also send them literature, letting them know that you need them and their support of the project. Perhaps in later stewardship education, you could address very briefly some of the reasons why people don't or haven't given and encourage them to do so. In a small church you might discuss their concerns about the church without directly confronting them about their failure to join the campaign.

Update Communication

Just as the church needs to communicate to keep the congregation informed prior to the campaign, it needs to continue the flow of information over the life of the commitment period. Answer such questions as:

When will we purchase the land?
When will construction begin?
Is construction on schedule?
When is the move-in date?
How much interim interest will be saved if they accelerate their gift?
How much have people given to date versus what has been pledged?
How close is the church to reaching the campaign top goal?

Answers to these and other questions, along with photographs of progress, will encourage the church members to fulfill their pledges and challenge those who have not yet given or pledged to join in.

As mentioned already, the building fund will benefit if the church's offering envelopes are printed in such a way that individuals can designate what part of their check goes to the general fund, the missions fund, and the campaign or building fund. If they are receiving these offering envelopes in the mail on a monthly basis, they are being reminded throughout the year that they need to be giving to all three funds.

A special envelope designed solely for the campaign can also be mailed out at the end of each year with a letter to encourage people to catch up on their campaign pledge or to give above and beyond their pledge if God has provided in an unanticipated way.

Finally, just as prayer was a vital part of the planning and the execution of the campaign, it needs to be in the follow-up phase. Keep the specific prayer concerns of the ongoing campaign before your people. Ask them to pray not only for the successful completion of the project, campaign pledges to be fulfilled, and new goals to be reached, but more important, that God's people will be changed as they experience the worship of giving![1]

Questions for Reflection, Discussion, and Application

1. Who is the best person in your church to do the follow-up for the campaign? Is it the pastor? Why or why not?
2. Whom will you plan to follow up? Will it be those who have made a commitment? If so, how will you follow them up?
3. Will you follow up people who are new to your church? If so, how will you follow them up?
4. Will you follow up those who have not made a commitment? If no, why not? If yes, how?
5. Do you plan to update your communication to your people? If not, why not? If so, how?

Appendix A

A Theology of Financial Stewardship

What does Scripture say to God's people and to the church and its leaders about giving? Does God expect his people to tithe? What does the Bible teach the church about finances?

We will begin by briefly looking at the concept of biblical stewardship in the Old Testament, for that is the foundation for and context in which to best understand financial stewardship. Then we'll move to financial stewardship in the Old Testament. Next we'll repeat this same pattern in the New Testament, focusing on the local church.

Financial Stewardship in the Old Testament

Biblical Stewardship

The Old Testament teaches that everything in heaven and on earth belongs to God as sovereign head over all (1 Chron. 29:11, 16; Ps. 24:1–2; 50:10–12; 89:11). This includes such things as wealth and honor (1 Chron. 29:12), people (Ps. 24:1–2), animals, birds, creatures of the fields (Ps. 50:10–11), and much more.

God has entrusted this as a stewardship to mankind beginning with Adam in Genesis. God's mission for Adam at the time of his creation was to fill, subdue, and rule over the earth (Gen. 1:28), and his instructions for Adam in the garden were to work and care for it (2:15). This stewardship wasn't negated by the fall, as God extended it ultimately to mankind (Ps. 8:3–9). Thus mankind was responsible to manage it and return a portion to God, the owner and master of all of it (1 Chron. 29:14).

Financial Stewardship

With this understanding of biblical stewardship in place, we're ready to explore what the Old Testament says about financial stewardship.

Money in General

The Old Testament doesn't say a lot about money, and much of what it teaches is found in the wisdom literature. For example, in Proverbs 17:16 the writer warns that money without wisdom is foolishness. Then in Ecclesiastes 5:10 he warns that if you never have enough money and are never satisfied, you have a serious problem with a love for money.

Material Blessing

The Old Testament generally teaches that God blesses materially those who honor him with their possessions (Prov. 3:9–10; 11:24–25). An example would be Abraham (Gen. 14:18–20). Proverbs 28:27 teaches that those who give to the poor will lack nothing. And Psalm 112:1–3 teaches that God blesses with wealth those who fear and obey his commands. However, books such as Proverbs present this as general truth for which there are exceptions. Later the Pharisees misused this general concept to hoard wealth and claim that it was a sign of their spiritual superiority and God's subsequent blessing in their lives. While God blesses his people with material wealth, Scripture also warns that they must not trust in their riches in place of him (Ps. 52:5–7). Finally, Psalm 37:25–26 states that righteous people are generous givers.

Tithing

The Old Testament teaches that tithing was a major aspect of Old Testament worship in general and stewardship in particular. The problem is that scholars disagree on what the Old Testament commands. For example, we know that under the law, the Hebrews were supposed to tithe their crops, herds, and flocks, but we don't know how much.

Before the Mosaic law, some gave a tithe. For example, in Genesis 14:20 Abraham gave a tithe of the spoils of victory to Melchizedek, king of Salem. And in Genesis 28:22 Jacob promised to give back to God a tenth of all that God gave him. Some use these two texts to teach that God's people tithed before as well as under the Mosaic law; therefore, they believe that the principle of tithing is eternally applicable to all of

God's people, regardless of when they live. They would argue from this that tithing is for today.

However, the practice of tithing is not what these passages are teaching. First, it's important to note that they are descriptive and not prescriptive passages. They are describing what took place back then, not prescribing what we should do today. Second, the point of the passages is not to instruct Israel or the church to tithe. For example, Moses recorded the events in Genesis 14:20 to show that God was with Abraham and that he was blessed of God, not to teach tithing. Abraham's tithe is incidental to the passage, not the point of the passage. The same is true of the Jacob narrative.

Under Mosaic law there may have been several mandatory tithes, but for some the actual number isn't clear. In his Bible dictionary, Merrill Unger writes that there were likely two tithes, possibly a third.[1] Richard Cunningham finds three different tithes in the Old Testament.[2] Some of the central texts on tithing in the Old Testament follow.

- A tithe of Israel's crops, herds, and flocks (Lev. 27:30–32; Deut. 12:4–18; 14:22–23).
- There may have been a second tithe of produce that was to go to the Levites who served at the Tent of Meeting (Num. 18:27–28). They needed these offerings because they had no inheritance in the land (vv. 21–24). However, some feel that this wasn't a second tithe, but part of the original tithe commanded in Leviticus 27 and Deuteronomy 12 and 14 that was given to the Levites. (Nehemiah 10:34–39 would seem to support the latter view.)
- There may have been a third tithe (a charity tithe) for the fatherless, aliens, and widows, taken every third year (Deut. 14:28–29; 26:12–13). It may, however, have been part of the tithe that was given to the Levites (Num. 18:21, 24; Deut. 14:28–29).
- From these passages we learn that we don't know with certainty how much the Hebrews tithed under law. They may have regularly tithed once or twice a year, and possibly a third time, every third year. Thus their giving would have ranged anywhere from 10 to 23 percent.

The importance of tithing was not the amount one tithed, but the fact that the practice of tithing was an act of worship, acknowledging Israel's stewardship and giving back to God a portion of what he had given to his people. It acknowledged God's ownership of the land and its produce, flocks, and herds. According to Malachi 3:8–10, not to give God any or all of his tithe was to rob him of what was his and to put oneself under a curse.

God instructed Israel to bring their tithes not to their own towns but to the place where the Lord was present (Deut. 12:5–7, 12, 17–18), which initially was the tabernacle (Exod. 33:7–11). Later this was the temple, and specifically the storehouse in the temple (Mal. 3:10) where the tithed grain was kept (Neh. 10:38; 13:12) and where the Levites and priests were responsible for it. Later we'll see that in the early church, the money was brought to God at the church where the apostles took responsibility for it (Acts 4:34–35).

As we saw above, the Jewish practice was to tithe their crops, herds, and flocks to the Lord. Keep in mind that the majority of Israelites were farmers. Theirs was primarily an agricultural economy. People of other professions, such as craftsmen and fishermen, didn't tithe. In the time of Christ, the Pharisees pushed this to an extreme, tithing everything that is eaten or grown (Matt. 23:23; Luke 11:42). And later the church fathers expanded the tithe to include all sources of one's income.

Financial Stewardship in the New Testament

Biblical Stewardship

The New Testament picks up on the stewardship theme and develops it further, providing the context for and teachings on financial stewardship.

The New Testament Greek word for steward, which is *oikonomos*, is rendered *manager* in the NIV translation of the New Testament. In the classical Greek it was used of a person (often a slave) who was responsible for and ran the affairs of a household for the master or owner of the house.

Jesus provides the primary teaching on stewardship in his parables found in the Gospels. He uses *oikonomos* (manager) twice, once in Luke 12:42 and again in Luke 16:1–13, to illustrate stewardship truths. In both passages he uses the term with the same meaning as that of classical Greek—a manager who is in charge of his master's household and estate while the master is away—to illustrate the importance of faithfulness to Jesus's call on his disciples' lives. Let's examine both passages.

The Parable of the Servants

In the first passage, Luke 12:42–48, Jesus tells the parable of the servants. Here Jesus uses the stewardship metaphor to call his disciples to be faithful followers, because unfaithfulness proves costly. The wise stewards in the parable are the disciples who work faithfully for God's people and look for the Lord's return. They will be rewarded accordingly (vv. 42–44).

Those disciples who for whatever reason don't serve him and are unfaithful will suffer adverse consequences, depending on the nature of their unfaithfulness (vv. 45–48). There are three types of unfaithful disciples. Those who are blatantly disobedient will experience rejection (vv. 45–46). Those who are consciously and willfully disobedient but not blatantly disobedient will suffer discipline (v. 47). And finally those who disobey in ignorance will suffer slight discipline (v. 48).

The Parable of the Shrewd Manager

In the parable of the shrewd manager (Luke 16:1–13), Jesus tells the parable and then makes three applications.

1. In verse 9 Jesus teaches that God has entrusted us as his steward-managers with his present, temporary resources (worldly wealth) to provide for future eternal relationships (true riches).
2. In verses 10–12 he cautions that if one is a poor steward-manager of little things, such as money, in this life, how can he expect great things of God in the life to come? Be faithful now (with finances), so that you will be given greater responsibility in the life to come.
3. In verse 13 he instructs us to make God, not money, the ultimate priority of our life.

Other Parables

Jesus's concept of stewardship is foundational to many of the other parables. You will find it embedded in the following parables, cited earlier in chapter 1 of this book: the unmerciful servant (Matt. 18:21–35), the workers in the vineyard (20:1–16), the two sons (21:28–32), the murderous tenants (vv. 33–44), the talents (25:14–30), the rich fool (Luke 12:16–21), the rich man and Lazarus (16:19–31), the unworthy servant (17:7–10), and the ten minas (19:11–27).

Financial Stewardship

With this further understanding of biblical stewardship, we are ready to turn to the New Testament teaching on financial stewardship.

Jesus's Key Teachings on Finances

The following treatment is not meant to be exhaustive but representative of Jesus's teachings on finances found primarily in the Gospels. These are instructive for Jesus's disciples in today's churches regarding their giving.

- *Jesus's disciples serve God, not money.* As we saw above in the parable of the shrewd manager (Luke 16:1–15), Jesus teaches us that it's impossible to serve two masters. We have to make a choice, and it's imperative that his disciples make God—not money—the ultimate priority of our lives.

- *Jesus's disciples give inconspicuously, not publicly.* In Matthew 6:1–4 Jesus teaches us an aspect of how to give. The context addresses the issue of how to act in such a way that God rewards one's religious activities of giving, prayer, and fasting (vv. 1–18). The disciple's motives are key. In verse 1 he warns that God will not reward some of us because of the way we carried out our religious duties. In verses 2–4 he addresses giving as a religious activity and teaches that God rewards one's giving when it's a private, personal matter between the giver and God, as opposed to a public display to win the praise of men.

- *Jesus's disciples invest in heavenly treasure, not earthly treasure.* In Matthew 6:19–24 Jesus teaches that what we do with our money says something about what we truly value in life. He exhorts his disciples to store up treasure in heaven (heavenly treasure), not on earth (earthly treasure), because where we store up our treasure reveals where our hearts are. His references to the heart and to treasure represent our priorities and values in life that ultimately affect our decisions. Are they set on this life or the life to come? While it's not wrong to have material things, Jesus asks if our focus is on them or on the life to come. We are loyal to what we value most. In other words, where do our true loyalties lie? The answer to this question will reveal our life's focus and where we are spiritually.

- *God provides for the material needs of Jesus's disciples.* Jesus's disciples may hesitate to give because they're worried about such common necessities of life as clothing and food. In Matthew 6:25–34 he addresses this concern. He commands us not to worry about such matters as the food we eat or the clothes we wear, because, if we put his kingdom and righteousness first (v. 33), he will provide for all of these needs. In addition, in Luke 6:38 Jesus tells his disciples that not only will God provide for their needs, but he'll bless their giving—"Give, and it will be given to you."

- *Jesus's disciples give in proportion to what they have.* Mark 12:41–44 tells the story of how on one occasion the rich were giving large amounts of money to the temple treasury, whereas a poor widow gave only two small coins worth little. Jesus uses the offering of this poor widow to address another key aspect of giving—how much one should give. In this story Jesus teaches that the amount one gives should be in proportion to what one has. More is expected from those who have much. Less is expected from those who have little. Though the widow gave less than the rich, she actually gave more from Jesus's perspective, because she had very little from which to give. The rich people, on the other hand, had much from which to give.

- *Jesus's disciples opt for giving over receiving.* Using Jesus's words, Paul reveals in Acts 20:35 what our attitude toward giving should be. Though not recorded in the Gospels, Paul tells us that Christ believed it is more blessed to give than receive. He opts for giving rather than receiving. The "one with the most toys" doesn't win. The blessings in our lives come not from what we get but from what we give.
- *Jesus's disciples may receive financial support.* In Luke 8:1–3 Luke informs his readers that Jesus, and likely the Twelve, received financial support during their touring ministry. Verse 2 tells us that not only did the Twelve accompany Jesus, but a group of women traveled with him as well. They had benefited from his ministry of exorcism and healing. These ladies not only accompanied Jesus and his disciples but helped support them from their own means (v. 3).

The Early Churches and Finances

The book of Acts is the church history book of the New Testament that provides us with a limited picture of how two early, young churches handled their finances and various issues related to them. We'll look at three primary texts. They focus on the church at Jerusalem (Acts 2 and 4–5), and the church at Antioch (Acts 11). Other passages such as 1 Corinthians 9 and 1 Timothy 5 also address financial aspects of the New Testament church. We'll briefly look at them as well.

As we examine these passages, we must remember two important points. First, we are working with narrative literature where we must be careful to distinguish between descriptive and prescriptive passages. These passages in Acts are descriptive and provide us with a limited picture of how certain churches handled their finances. However, we must not use their practices prescriptively, making them mandatory for all churches for all times, unless there is some evidence in the text or some other passages in the Bible that indicate we are to do so.

Second, we must not assume that all churches handled their finances in the same way. Just because the church at Jerusalem held all things in common doesn't necessarily mean that the church at Antioch or other churches did the same, unless we find evidence in the Bible of it.

The first primary text is Acts 2:41–47. This is one of several church progress reports that Luke presents in the book (see 6:7; 9:31; 12:24; 16:5; 19:20; 28:30–31). In this first progress report, Luke provides us with a brief summary of how the Jerusalem church was doing. Here he also gives us a glimpse of how the Jerusalem church used its finances. In verses 44–45 he writes: "All the believers were together and had everything in common. Selling their possessions and goods, they gave to anyone as he had need." In particular we discover how the early church dealt with those who were needy.

In verse 44 he tells us that the early believers were together, meaning that they were in harmony with one another; they had a strong sense of unity. Then Luke adds that this led to their having "everything in common." This he explains in verse 45, where he tells us that people would sell what they owned (their possessions and goods) and give the proceeds to those among them who were in need. (Here the imperfect tense signals that this was a recurrent but likely ad hoc practice that took place whenever anyone had need.)

This passage is not teaching that individuals in the church gave up their ownership of property to the church or that all in the church should be equal or that this practice was mandatory for all. (Later in Acts 5:4 Luke makes it very clear that the one who gave property—or in this case, land—was its rightful owner and was free to dispose of it as he or she wanted.) This passage is teaching that the people were willing to liquidate such assets to help those with legitimate needs. Perhaps an example of such need is found in Acts 6:1, where we find that the church was involved in distributing food to its needy widows. These early Christians felt that people were more important than their possessions, and they were willing to put people ahead of their possessions.

In the next primary passage, Acts 4:32–5:14, Luke again emphasizes how the young church was unified as manifest by people's willingness to share their personal possessions and to sell off land and houses to meet the needs of others. Luke uses Barnabas as a positive example (4:36–37), and Ananias and Sapphira as negative examples (5:1–11), to address people's proper and improper motives for giving.

Ananias and Sapphira were guilty of selfish deception because they sold a piece of property and supposedly brought the money to the church, somehow giving everyone the impression that they had given all of the proceeds. The truth was they had held back some of the money for themselves. Peter addresses their sin and Ananias dies suddenly, followed shortly by his wife. This might seem harsh, but it is likely that the couple's behavior threatened the unity the body of believers was experiencing, and so God dealt with them by taking their lives.

In this account Luke also gives us some insight as to who in the church handled the money from the sales and how they handled it. In 4:34–35 we learn that people brought their money to the "apostles' feet." The same statement is made in verse 37 and in 5:2. In his commentary Ben Witherington writes that this practice was Semitic and an act of submission to apostolic authority, and that the apostles, in turn, took responsibility for the proper distribution of the funds.[3] This makes sense in light of what took place later in Acts 6:1–7, where the Twelve apparently shifted the responsibility for this distribution to other qualified people. While this practice is descriptive, not prescriptive, it indicates that the funds were to be handled by those with leadership authority, which makes perfect sense.

We discovered above that in the Old Testament, a good Jew brought his or her tithe to the tabernacle and later the temple, where it was placed in a storage room under the supervision of the Levites and priests for later distribution. In the New Testament the members of the early church brought their money to the apostles who were responsible to distribute it to the needy, until they handed this responsibility off to other qualified people. Though descriptive, not prescriptive, and thus not mandatory, this would seem to teach that a wise practice for believers is to give their money to the church, where those with leadership authority will see to its proper use on behalf of the entire body.

In Acts 11:27–30 we find one further reference to the church and finances. In verses 27–28 Luke presents a problem that the new church in Antioch addressed. Agabus, one of several prophets from Jerusalem, came to the church in Antioch and predicted a severe famine that would affect the Jerusalem church. The believers at Antioch decided that they would provide help for the believers living in Judea. Here we discover five practices.

1. They seem to have raised these funds from individuals within the church rather than take them from some established fund of the church.
2. The amount was based on the individual's ability to give (v. 29) and not some set amount.
3. They gave this money specifically to believers. Verse 29 says, "to provide help for the brothers." The practice of the Jerusalem and Antioch churches appears to have been for believers (2:44–45; 4:34). Does this mean that they didn't help the poor who were unbelievers? I suspect that there were times when they helped unbelievers as well. However, the text simply doesn't address this.
4. They sent their gifts to the elders, who may have been the pastors in Judea. This seems to be similar to the practice of the Jerusalem

church that gave their funds to their leaders for distribution (Acts 4:34–35, 37; 5:2). This may have been a strategic move to make sure the funds were used as intended.

5. They sent their gift by Barnabas and Saul, who were sent out by the Jerusalem church to minister to the church at Antioch. At first this might seem like an act of convenience—they were going in that direction, why not send it with them? However, I suspect it also reflected the apostles' desire that the distribution of the money be handled in a proper, aboveboard manner, as Paul mentions in 1 Corinthians 16:2–4 and 2 Corinthians 8:18–21.

Again, this text is descriptive and shows the care and concern that believers had for one another in the first century. However, it's not laying down any mandatory, formal practices for today's church. A church might attempt to follow a similar practice today, but it would be wrong to insist that the practice is biblically mandated and that those who do it differently are wrong.

Before we leave this section on the early church and its finances, we want to touch briefly on the church's remuneration of those involved in its ministry. Is it okay for churches to pay some of those who serve in its ministry? For instance, is it okay to pay the pastor a salary for his services? Acts doesn't comment on remuneration in the early churches at Jerusalem and Antioch. However, Paul addresses the issue of remuneration in writing to some of the churches that he planted later while on his missionary journeys. We'll find the bulk of his teaching in 1 Corinthians 9 and 1 Timothy 5:17–18.

Both passages quote Deuteronomy 25:4—"Do not muzzle an ox while it is treading out the grain"—to support Paul's teaching that "the worker deserves his wages" (1 Tim. 5:18). The context of both passages addresses remunerating those who were fully involved in serving the church (in this case the church of Corinth and those churches to whom Timothy ministered). Paul argues strongly that he has the right to be remunerated by the Corinthians for his ministry to and for them. But he has chosen to waive this right in light of some of the false accusations that he was "in ministry for the money" (1 Cor. 9:3–6). Then in 1 Timothy 5:17 Paul instructs Timothy that it's important that the church remunerate those who "direct the affairs of the church." He is referring to the elders, who most likely were the first-century equivalent to today's full-time pastors. Besides this principle that the laborer is worthy of his hire, Scripture is silent on whom the church should pay and how it is to do so. These questions are left up to each church to decide on its own.

What might we conclude about what is said—and the fact that so little is said in Acts and other passages about the church and its finances?

First, what is said? We discovered several practices from the Jerusalem and Antioch churches, the church at Corinth, and those to whom Timothy ministered:

1. The Jerusalem church took care of its needy people (Acts 2:42–47; 4:32–5:10).
2. On occasion a church (Antioch) helped another church (Jerusalem) in need (Acts 11:27–30). The churches of Galatia and the church at Corinth did the same (1 Cor. 16:1–4).
3. The church helped believers (Acts 2:44–45; 4:34; 11:29). Scripture is silent on whether the church helped unbelievers.
4. The church entrusted its finances to its leadership (Acts 4:34–35) and to other leaders (11:30) for proper care and distribution.
5. The church was to remunerate its full-time people (1 Cor. 9:11–12; 1 Tim. 5:17–18).

As pointed out above, we must move with caution because the texts are descriptive not prescriptive. We argue that as long as a church doesn't violate Scripture, the lack of instruction implies that a church is free under the Holy Spirit's direction to handle these matters in wisdom as they see fit. An example would be the church's decision to help an unbelieving family in need who is not part of the church.

We must not assume that all the early churches handled finances in the same way that the Jerusalem church did in Acts 2 and 4, the Antioch church did in Acts 11, or the Corinthian church did in 1 Corinthians 16:1–4. If we do, we impose on today's churches what we believe the early church practiced, and we have no biblical justification.

Paul's teaching on financial remuneration of those involved in the church's ministry, however, is different. Rather than merely describing what the churches did or didn't do, Paul is clear in both 1 Corinthians 9 and 1 Timothy 5 that the church has a responsibility to remunerate its people in ministry, most likely full-time ministry.

Paul's Teaching on Giving

We want to focus on several Pauline passages that are most instructive for churches concerning biblical giving. Romans 12:6–8 and 2 Corinthians 8–9 are important in this regard.

Romans 12:6–8

In Romans 12:6–8 Paul teaches that some have a gift of giving that involves their contributing generously to the needs of others. He writes,

"We have different gifts, according to the grace given us. . . . If it is contributing to the needs of others, let him give generously." This passage addresses the church's ministry through the exercise of its members' spiritual gifts, identifying some of these gifts or abilities and encouraging their exercise. In verse 8 he mentions four gifts: encouraging, contributing, leading, and showing mercy. The gift of contributing focuses specifically on giving of what one has to those in need.

We can gain additional insight into this passage from Ephesians 4:28 where similar terminology is used. The term for *contributing* used here in Romans 12:8 is the same term Paul uses in Ephesians 4:28, where the NIV translates it as *share*—"He who has been stealing must steal no longer, but must work, doing something useful with his own hands, that he may have something to share with those in need." Here the implication is that people should work so that they can provide for the needy (likely money). Paul assumes that there are those in the church, the body of Christ, who have a gift of giving, specifically to the needy person. His command further addresses how these gifted believers are to exercise their gift of giving. They are to do so generously.

2 Corinthians 8–9

In Paul's letters to the Corinthians, he says more about money and giving than in any of his other epistles (especially in 2 Corinthians 8–9). Paul has been involved with organizing a collection for the poor in Jerusalem (Gal. 2:10). The church at Corinth had wanted to be a part of this fund-raising effort (1 Cor. 16:1–2) but somehow they had not followed through in their giving. Thus in 2 Corinthians 8–9 Paul urges the church to fulfill their commitment through generous giving.

In these two chapters on gracious giving, he addresses three key areas of New Testament giving in the context of the church: how to give, how much to give, and the benefits of giving. First, let's examine Paul's teaching on *how* to give. How are Christians to give? What should be their attitude toward giving? The following are snippets that briefly detail Paul's teaching on how to give.

> *Give generously.* In 2 Corinthians 8:3–5 Paul uses the example of the churches in Macedonia to teach that giving is to be done generously. He writes in verse 3: "For I testify that they gave as much as they were able, and even beyond their ability." Then in 2 Corinthians 9:6 Paul says that giving is to be done generously and not grudgingly.
>
> *Give regularly/systematically.* In 1 Corinthians 16:2 Paul teaches the Corinthians to give regularly or systematically. In their case this was to be on the first day of every week. However, he's not emphasizing

when but how often. (In light of his teaching in Romans 14:5–12, I highly doubt that Paul would refuse to accept a gift if it were collected at another time.)

Give proportionately. Here Paul says that giving should be proportionate. He writes: "each one of you should set aside a sum of money in keeping with his income" (1 Cor. 16:2). And again in 2 Corinthians 8:11–12, he encourages that their giving be "according to your means. For if the willingness is there, the gift is acceptable according to what one has, not according to what he does not have." (In Mark 12:43–44 Jesus contrasts the small offering of a poor widow with the gift of the rich to teach the same lesson.)

Give sacrificially. In 2 Corinthians 8:5 Paul adds, "but they gave themselves first to the Lord and then to us in keeping with God's will." Their giving involved the sacrifice of themselves to God and then to those to whom they were giving.

Give willingly. In 2 Corinthians 8:11 Paul compliments his readers on their "eager willingness" to give and encourages them to follow through on their commitment.

Give voluntarily. In 2 Corinthians 9:7 Paul writes: "Each man should give what he has decided in his heart to give, not reluctantly or under compulsion." Giving that comes from the heart and is not done with reluctance or under pressure is voluntary giving.

Give cheerfully. Paul encourages giving cheerfully when he says, "God loves a cheerful giver" (2 Cor. 9:7).

Give eagerly. In 2 Corinthians 8:10–11 Paul mentions the eager willingness of the Corinthians to give. Then in 2 Corinthians 9:2 Paul compliments the church because of its eagerness to give and even boasts about it to other churches.

Give enthusiastically. Paul refers to how the Corinthians' enthusiasm to give has stirred others to follow suit (2 Cor. 9:2).

Give excellently. In 2 Corinthians 8:7 Paul commands that his readers excel at giving. He wants them to be good at it, just as they are good at other things.

Give strategically. It would appear that the church's giving was done strategically, in the sense that it was accomplishing something worthwhile for the kingdom that would have kingdom impact and make a difference for the cause of Christ, as opposed to something that wasn't making a difference. Paul says the gift will result in praise to God as well as helping those in need (2 Cor. 9:12–15).

Give scrupulously. Paul explains to the church in 2 Corinthians 8:18–21 that other respected, approved people will be involved in the delivery and administration of their gift. The reason is found in verses 20–21: "We want to avoid any criticism of the way we administer this liberal gift. For we are taking pains to do what is right, not only in the eyes of the Lord but also in the eyes of men." This same concern is reflected in Paul's instructions in 1 Corinthians 16:3–4.

Paul's Teaching on How to Give

Generously	2 Cor. 8:2–4; 9:6
Regularly/systematically	1 Cor. 16:2
Proportionately	1 Cor. 16:2; 2 Cor. 8:11–12
Sacrificially	2 Cor. 8:3–5
Willingly	2 Cor. 8:11–12
Voluntarily	2 Cor. 9:7
Cheerfully	2 Cor. 9:7
Eagerly	2 Cor. 8:10–11; 9:2
Enthusiastically	2 Cor. 9:2
Excellently	2 Cor. 8:7
Strategically	2 Cor. 9:12–15
Scrupulously	1 Cor. 16:3–4; 2 Cor. 8:18–21

Now let's look at Paul's teaching on *how much* to give. This is a question in every believer's mind. What does God expect? What or how much is good giving?

Give a proportional amount. As we saw above, the amount one gives should be in keeping with one's income (1 Cor. 16:2), according to one's means (2 Cor. 8:11), and according to what one has, not what he doesn't have (v. 12). Thus how much you give should be in proportion to what you have.

Give a generous amount. In 2 Corinthians 8:2 Paul commends the Macedonian churches for their generosity. He explains in verse 3: "For I testify that they gave as much as they were able." Then in 2 Corinthians 9:5 he gives the church advice on how to arrange for the giving of their gift so that it would be generous. And he reminds them in verses 6 and 10–11 of the importance of giving a generous amount.

Give a heartfelt amount. In 2 Corinthians 9:7 Paul instructs: "Each man should give what he has decided in his heart to give." He doesn't specify an amount, but says it should be a heartfelt amount—what you have decided in your heart to give.

Give a sacrificial amount. Not only does Paul say that the Macedonian churches gave generously, but in 2 Corinthians 8:3 he adds that they were willing to go even further: "For I testify that they gave as much as they were able, and even beyond their ability." Giving beyond one's ability is sacrificial giving. A distinction should be made between normal, regular giving that honors God and sacrificial giving. There are times in the lives of our churches that the congregation needs to give over and above what is normal, good giving to address particular needs, such as missions, facilities expansion, or new facilities to handle growth challenges, as well as other situations.

Paul's Teaching on How Much to Give

A proportional amount	1 Cor. 16:2; 2 Cor. 8:11–12
A generous amount	2 Cor. 8:2–3; 9:5–6, 11
A heartfelt amount	2 Cor. 9:7
A sacrificial amount	2 Cor. 8:3

Finally, let's examine Paul's teaching on the benefits of giving. In 2 Corinthians 9:6–15, Paul explains that there are at least three benefits to good giving.

1. We discover that God graciously enriches good givers (2 Cor. 9:6–11). If you give generously, God will bless you generously. (This is also the message of Proverbs 3:9–10 and 11:24–25.) When you are generous, you will have all that you need so that you can be even more generous. This is likely the idea behind Paul's comments on finances in Philippians 4:10–20, where he says in verse 19: "And my God will meet all your needs according to his glorious riches in Christ Jesus."
2. Paul teaches that our good giving supplies the needs of God's people (2 Cor. 9:12a). The goal according to 2 Corinthians 8:13–15 is equality—no extremes of poverty or wealth among God's people. Most likely this is similar to what the early church experienced in Acts 2 and 4, where it says that they had everything in common. Those with wealth gave to help those in poverty.
3. Our good giving leads others to praise God (2 Cor. 9:12b–15). The implication seems to be that as we help others, they in turn see that God is truly the one supplying their needs and so they give God the praise he deserves.

Paul's Teaching on the Benefits of Good Giving

God's generous blessing	2 Cor. 9:6–11
The supply of people's needs	2 Cor. 9:12a
Praise to God	2 Cor. 9:12b–15

The Tithe

There is still the question of the tithe. Should we give a tithe? The New Testament doesn't prescribe or mandate that Christians under grace must tithe. While it mentions tithing three times (Matt. 23:23; Luke 18:12; Heb. 7:1–10), all three references are incidental to other teachings and don't teach or require tithing as a New Testament practice. Also tithing was mandated and practiced under Mosaic law, and believers are not under law (Rom. 10:4, Eph. 2:14–15, Heb. 8:13) but under grace (Gal. 3:1–25). Giving is an act of grace (2 Cor. 8:6–7), under grace. Consequently the believer under grace has freedom to give as he or she desires, according to what we have learned in 2 Corinthians 8–9. If one insists that tithing is still to be practiced today, it must be determined how much one should tithe. This study of tithing under the Mosaic law reveals that it is not clear on the total amount, because there may have been several mandatory tithes. It could have ranged anywhere from 10 to 23 percent.

Many Christians, especially new ones, want to know what is good giving under grace. How much should they give to honor God? We advise them that, though the New Testament in general and grace giving in particular don't mandate a tithe, it was good giving in the Old Testament under law and is a good place to start, as long as we don't get legalistic about it. Since the word *tithe* means "a tenth," many say that one-tenth is the "threshold" or suggested starting point for giving—even under grace.

Other Teaching on Finances

While Paul provides us with much of our New Testament teaching on finances, others address the issue as well. In particular James and John address aspects that affect the local church.

James, the half brother of Jesus, addresses finances in James 2:1–13. In a hypothetical illustration, he talks about those who come into the believer's meeting. Most likely this is a synagogue, but the same truth would seem to apply to any meeting of believers, whether a synagogue or church. What's the message? Simply put, he warns the readers not to favor those with financial means (the rich) over the poor.

John explains that those who went out to minister on behalf of the Name (most likely Jesus's name) didn't solicit help from the pagans or those who were unbelievers (3 John 5–8). The point is they are to be supported by God's people in the church, not by those to whom they were sent to bear witness for Christ.

Appendix B

Precampaign Questionnaire

Please answer each question below to the best of your ability. Your answers are vital in helping the Malphurs Group know how to serve you.

1. Where is your church located (town, city, etc.)? Are you in a rural, suburban, or urban area? What's the nearest large metropolitan center? How far are you away from the nearest large airport?
2. How old is the church? Has it ever relocated? If so, when and from where?
3. How long has the senior pastor been at the church? What is his background, education, family? What is his age? What are his spiritual gifts? What other churches has he pastored? What is his email address and what are his phone numbers where he can be reached (cell, home, and church numbers)?
4. How many staff do you have? Who are they, what do they do, and what are their backgrounds? How many are full-time?
5. Does the church have a governing board? If so, is it a deacon or elder board? If neither of these, what kind of board is it? Does the church have a patriarch or matriarch?
6. What is the church's polity (congregational, episcopal, presbyterian, etc.)?
7. Has the church been through a strategic planning process? If so, when and did they work with a consultant?
8. Does the church have a list of core values, a mission statement, and a vision statement? If so, what are they?
9. What are some of the church's ministries (worship service, Sunday school, small groups, adult Bible fellowships, Awana, etc.)?
10. Would you describe your church as more traditional or contemporary? Why?

11. Is your worship style more contemporary, traditional, or blended?
12. How many services do you have on a typical weekend?
13. What are the church's biggest strengths and weaknesses?
14. On a scale of 1 to 10 (1 being low and 10 high), how evangelistic is your church?
15. What is the church's average worship attendance at its services?
16. Is the church growing, plateaued, or declining in numbers? Why? What is the church's numerical growth goal? How large would it like to become? Why?
17. What is the size of your property in acres? How much of it is usable acreage? What is the number of parking spaces? Do you have a gymnasium? Do you believe that you have enough room? Why or why not?
18. How many people can you seat in your auditorium? Do you have chairs or pews?
19. What is the church's total annual giving over the last four or five years? Is it growing, plateaued, or declining?
20. What is the church's total budget? Will you provide us with a copy of your budget? How much money has the church budgeted for facilities?
21. What are the church's assets?
22. What is the church's current total indebtedness? What is it for (mortgage payment, vehicles, etc.)? Does the church have a mortgage?
23. Have you or the church ever been involved in a capital campaign before? If so, how many and when? Why do you want to have a capital campaign?
24. Why do you need to raise funds (for land, a new facility, land and facility, missions, debt reduction, etc.)?
25. How much do you expect to raise from the campaign?
26. Does the congregation seem to be in favor of a capital campaign and understand the reasons for having one? How do you know?
27. Has the church ever worked with a consultant before? If so, when, why, and with whom?
28. Does the church have a logo, a preferred color and/or font for its name, a website (give website address)? Please provide a copy of any logo or name format. How does the church publicize itself (mailers, radio ads, etc.)?
29. What else should we know about you or your congregation?

The Malphurs Group
7916 Briar Brook Ct., Dallas, TX 75218
Cell: 469–585–2102 Fax: 214–327–1753
Aubrey@dts.edu

Appendix C

Campaign Position Descriptions

Chairperson, Leadership Team

1. Pray for your own participation in the campaign.
2. Participate in the campaign by giving a sacrificial gift and a three-year pledge.
3. Let others know of your enthusiastic support for this endeavor.
4. Keep the campaign calendar on schedule.
5. Join the pastor at key contributor meal meetings when possible.
6. Serve as master of ceremonies at home advance briefings.
7. Give a testimony concerning your own stewardship and commitment to the campaign at a worship service and at all the advance briefings.
8. Collect, tabulate, and follow up on advance commitments including staff, leadership team, finance committee, church board, and small-group leaders.
9. Announce the advance pledge total and Victory Day total.
10. Lead follow-up efforts for three years.
11. Oversee the process and make sure the team members are doing their jobs.

Advance Gift Coordinator

1. Pray for your own participation in the campaign.
2. Participate in the campaign by giving a sacrificial gift and a three-year pledge.

3. Let others know of your enthusiastic support for this endeavor.
4. Work with the chairman of the leadership team to collect and tabulate advance commitments from the staff, leadership team, finance committee, church board, and Sunday school or small-group leaders.
5. Work with the pastor to solicit gifts from sources other than church members.
6. Recruit a team, as appropriate, to accomplish these tasks.

Children's Ministry Leader

1. Pray for your own participation in the campaign.
2. Participate in the campaign by giving a sacrificial gift and a three-year pledge.
3. Let others know of your enthusiastic support for this endeavor.
4. Work with staff members to ensure there is childcare (for children through third grade) at the church for the advance briefings.
5. Develop and implement a strategy to involve the children in the capital fund-raising drive. Possible ideas are: (1) have an on-going contest among the different grade levels with children bringing loose change and keeping a running total of what grade has brought the greatest amount or the greatest weight of coins; (2) have the children color pictures of what they think the church might look like one day; (3) have the children write letters to the architect who is designing the building to tell him or her what they would like to have included in the site plan.
6. Be prepared to present a check to the pastor on Vision Sunday for the total amount the children's division has raised to-date toward the project.
7. Recruit a team, as appropriate, to accomplish these tasks.

Graphics and Printing Coordinator

1. Pray for your own participation in the campaign.
2. Participate in the campaign by giving a sacrificial gift and a three-year pledge.
3. Let others know of your enthusiastic support for this endeavor.
4. Prepare graphics for all print pieces.
5. Get bids from printers for all print pieces.
6. Select printer and confirm lead times required for the pieces to be used in the campaign.
7. Check on the progress of all print jobs and confirm delivery, storage, and utilization of all materials.

Hospitality Coordinator

1. Pray for your own participation in the campaign.
2. Participate in the campaign by giving a sacrificial gift and a three-year pledge.
3. Let others know of your enthusiastic support for this endeavor.
4. Secure homes or other locations for the advance briefing meetings. The homes should be large enough to hold thirty people comfortably.
5. Hire a caterer to provide hors d'oeuvres and drinks (iced tea, coffee) to all advance briefings. The church will pay for the catering, and the host homes should not be responsible for any of the catering expense. The pastor or his designate should approve the contract for the caterer before it is signed.
6. Prepare name tags for the individuals who will attend the advance briefings. Be sure to have extra blank name tags on hand.
7. Arrange for a table at the front door where someone will greet people and hand out name tags.
8. Arrange for an additional twenty folding chairs to be at the advance briefings in case there is not adequate seating.
9. Make sure there is an easel at each advance briefing home so that a presentation may be displayed. There should also be a DVD player and television so that all attending can view a presentation.
10. Be present at all advance briefings to ensure the caterer is doing his or her job and that there is proper cleanup following the meeting. Arrive at the home at the same time the caterer arrives.
11. Record the names of those who attend the advance briefings.
12. Send a proper thank-you note to those who hosted the advance briefings.
13. Recruit a team, as appropriate, to accomplish these tasks.

Media Coordinator

1. Pray for your own participation in the campaign.
2. Participate in the campaign by giving a sacrificial gift and a three-year pledge.
3. Let others know of your enthusiastic support for this endeavor.
4. Ensure that three campaign DVDs are produced before the prescribed time on the campaign calendar. *Video One* will be shown at the advance briefing meetings. The video should be approximately three minutes in length, and its purpose is to inspire rather than

inform. You may include aerial shots of the community showing the great need, the construction going on, people moving in, people walking around, people attending worship at the church, aerial views of land, and so on. There should be background music and the voice of someone saying something like "God has called us to reach this community for Christ. He has blessed us with growth, and it is time now to prepare a home for the church. It is time now for God's people to step up . . ."

Video Two will be played in homes during prayer meetings and will basically be the senior pastor doing a heart-to-heart talk to the small group gathered in the home to pray about the campaign. Some of the same images that were in the advance briefing video can be used in this one as well. The purpose of this video is basically to present a challenge from the pastor. It can include music for inspiration. The length will be determined by how much the pastor wants to say in challenging the group. You probably don't want just a talking head. The pastor should be standing in an area where the future church building will be located.

Video Three will be shown on Vision Sunday during the worship service. This is the weekend prior to Commitment Day. Many people will not yet have seen a video, so this video will have some of the images you have already used in the first two videos. You should use different music, a different order of the images, and a different format for the images. In addition, this video will include information explaining the campaign and what it is trying to accomplish, the campaign goals, how to fill out the commitment card, and so on. It will probably be a little longer than the other videos, perhaps even six minutes in length. This will be determined by the amount of material you are trying to communicate and how long it takes to communicate this information, as well as what creative elements the pastor wants to include.

5. Make sure that all sound and video needs are met at all campaign events.

Phone Team Leader

1. Pray for your own participation in the campaign.
2. Participate in the campaign by giving a sacrificial gift and a three-year pledge.
3. Let others know of your enthusiastic support for this endeavor.
4. Enlist a sufficient number of individuals to serve on the phone team.

5. Ensure that all phone team members are present for the phone team training.
6. Compile the information garnered from the phone calls, giving special attention to those who have chosen to attend a different advance briefing site on a different date. Work with the church staff to ensure that new invitations are sent that reflect these changes.
7. Lead a second team to make follow-up calls to those the first phone team was unable to reach.

Prayer Team Leader

1. Pray for your own participation in the campaign.
2. Participate in the campaign by giving a sacrificial gift and a three-year pledge.
3. Let others know of your enthusiastic support for this endeavor.
4. Serve as the point person to keep prayer central in the campaign.
5. Make sure that every small group schedules a home prayer meeting sometime two to three weeks prior to Vision Sunday and Commitment Day.
6. Make sure that the youth group schedules a prayer meeting sometime during the same time period.
7. Make sure that all preschool teachers and children's teachers schedule prayer meetings during the same time period.
8. Work with the church staff to be sure there is a different prayer request related to the campaign in the weekly bulletin beginning six weeks prior to Vision Sunday and continuing through the end of the campaign.
9. Recruit a team, as appropriate, to accomplish these tasks.

Stewardship Education Leader

1. Pray for your own participation in the campaign.
2. Participate in the campaign by giving a sacrificial gift and a three-year pledge.
3. Let others know of your enthusiastic support for this endeavor.
4. Work with the staff in coordinating the small-group lesson on stewardship six to eight weeks before Vision Sunday.
5. Coordinate the follow-up through Sunday school.
6. Work with staff to ensure that all Sunday school leaders attend the training session.

7. Work with the pastor to secure testimonies for worship services on the three weekends prior to Vision Sunday. The capital leadership team chairman should give one of the testimonies.
8. Recruit a team, as appropriate, to accomplish these tasks.

Youth Ministry Leader

1. Pray for your own participation in the campaign.
2. Participate in the campaign by giving a sacrificial gift and a three-year pledge.
3. Let others know of your enthusiastic support for this endeavor.
4. Develop and implement a strategy for the youth ministry to be involved in the capital fund-raising campaign.
5. Cast a vision for the youth to make initial gifts and a three-year plan just like other church members.
6. Plan possible youth events where they can raise money as a group and/or as individuals—car washes, babysitting co-op, youth auction where young people can be hired to do odd jobs, etc.
7. Recruit a team, as appropriate, to accomplish these tasks.

Appendix D

Campaign Calendar

The dates in the sample campaign schedule below are based on a campaign with a commitment date of October 29, 2006. This target date (Commitment Sunday) is used as the reference point for scheduling all preceding events and tasks to be completed.

June

June 21: Train capital leadership team, graphics persons, and media persons

NOTE: Several months before this first month of the campaign, pastor begins key contributor meals with at least the top thirty givers. Training noted above begins eighteen weeks or four-and-a-half months before Commitment Sunday.

July

July 10: Advance briefing homes finalized

July 24: Advance briefing invitations to printer

August

August 1: Pastor letter #1*

August 3: Advance briefing invitations back from printer

August 7: Basic print package to printer

August 11: Mail advance briefing invitations

August 15: Capital leadership team phone training

August 17: First phone team begins

August 20: Stewardship message #1

August 21: Artist renderings due

August 22: Newsletter #1 to printer

August 25: Basic print package back from printer

August 27: Phone team reports / Stewardship message #2

August 28: Second phone team begins

August 31: New advance briefing invitations mailed

*Pastor letter #1 is sent to all church members to introduce the campaign and ask that they begin to pray about the campaign and their participation.

September

September 1: Newsletter #1 back from printer

September 5: Catering for advance briefings confirmed

September 6: DVD for advance briefings complete

September 7: Displays for advance briefings complete

September 8: Newsletter #1 mailed

September 10: Sunday school lesson

September 12: Capital leadership team meeting / First advance briefing

September 17: Sunday school lesson

September 18: Deadline for home prayer meeting dates and locations

September 24: Displays go up in foyer / Sunday school lesson

September 25: Newsletter #2 to Printer

September 26: DVD for home prayer meetings complete

September 27: Pastor letter #2*

Note: Advance briefings to be scheduled from September 12–24

*Pastor letter #2 is sent to those who were invited to but did not attend an advance briefing, asking them to consider participating and making an advance gift.

October

October 1: Testimony and message / Sunday school lesson

October 3: Newsletter #2 back from printer

October 5: Advance pledge reminder / Pastor letter #3*

October 8: Testimony and message / Sunday school lesson

October 9: Newsletter #2 mailed

October 10: Home prayer meetings October 8–15

October 11: Email reminder for advance pledge

October 15: Testimony and message / Sunday school lesson / Advance pledge deadline

October 16: DVD for Vision Sunday complete

October 20: Pledge cards and pastor letter #4† mailed

October 22: Vision Sunday

October 26: Email reminders sent about Commitment Sunday

October 29: Commitment Sunday

October 31: Pledge cards and pastor letter #5‡ mailed to non-participants

*Pastor letter #3 is sent to all advance briefing invitees who have not turned in an advance commitment card, reminding them about Vision Sunday and asking that they consider making an advance commitment.

†Pastor letter #4 is sent to members (and a slightly different letter to nonmember regular attenders) to remind them of Commitment Sunday, and is enclosed with a commitment card, return envelope, and offering envelope.

‡Pastor letter #5 is sent to members from whom a commitment was not received, asking them to consider participating (worded in a way that suggests it could have gone to all members as a reminder).

November

November 5: Sunday school follow-up

November 12: Victory Sunday / Sunday school follow-up

December

December 26: Pastor letter #6 sent as a reminder of the New Year and new commitment

December 29: Email sent as a reminder of the New Year and new commitment

Notes

Introduction

1. Dick Towner, "Money Management That Makes Sense," *Church Executive* (July 2005), http://www.churchexecutive.com/.
2. "Americans Donate Billions to Charity, but Giving to Churches Has Declined," Barna Research Online, April 25, 2005, http://www.barna.org, p. 1.
3. Ibid.
4. Ibid., 2.
5. Ibid., 2–3.
6. Ibid., 3.

Chapter 2 Developing Donors

1. Bill Hybels, *Courageous Leadership* (Grand Rapids: Zondervan, 2002), 98.
2. George Barna, *How to Increase Giving in Your Church* (Ventura, CA: Regal, 1997), 92–93.
3. Randy Alcorn, *The Treasure Principle* (Sisters, OR: Multnomah, 2001).
4. Aubrey Malphurs, *Advanced Strategic Planning*, 2nd. ed. (Grand Rapids: Baker, 2005).
5. Barna, *How to Increase Giving*, 118.
6. "God, Money, and the Pastor," *Leadership Journal* (Fall 2002), 30–31.

Chapter 4 Developing a Strategic Budget

1. "God, Money, and the Pastor," 27.

Chapter 5 Analyzing Your Strategic Budget

1. Aubrey Malphurs, *Values-Driven Leadership*, 2nd ed. (Grand Rapids: Baker, 2005).
2. "God, Money, and the Pastor," 27.

Chapter 6 Deciding Who Decides

1. Charles C. Ryrie, *A Survey of Bible Doctrine* (Chicago: Moody, 1972), 148.
2. Aubrey Malphurs, *Leading Leaders* (Grand Rapids: Baker, 2005).

Chapter 9 Understanding Good Banking Basics

1. Steve and Aubrey want to thank and give full credit to Gary L. Tipton, the president and CEO of Inwood Bank in Dallas, Texas, and a member of our church, for most of the information in this section as well as his valuable insight and input throughout this chapter.

Chapter 11 Keeping It Legal

1. Julie L. Bloss, J.D., CEBS, *The Church Guide to Employment Law,* 2nd ed. (Matthews, NC: Christian Ministry Resources, 1999).

Chapter 13 Preparing for a Capital Campaign

1. Aubrey Malphurs, *Developing a Vision for Ministry in the Twenty-first Century* (Grand Rapids: Baker, 1999).

Chapter 15 Following Up the Campaign

1. In 2006 Steve Stroope conducted a "Lead Your Own Capital Campaign" workshop. If you are interested in more information on capital campaigns, the four-hour video of this workshop will be helpful. For information on purchasing the video, contact strategic@lakepointe.org.

Appendix A A Theology of Financial Stewardship

1. Merrill F. Unger, *Unger's Bible Dictionary* (Chicago: Moody Press, 1963), 1103.
2. Richard B. Cunningham, "The Purpose of Stewardship," in *Leadership Handbooks of Practical Theology*, ed. James D. Berkley (Grand Rapids: Baker, 1994), 3:407.
3. Ben Witherington III, *The Acts of the Apostles: A Socio-Rhetorical Commentary* (Grand Rapids: Eerdmans, 1998), 208.

Index

Aubrey Malphurs (PhD, Dallas Theological Seminary) is professor of pastoral ministries at Dallas Theological Seminary. A nationally recognized expert on leadership issues, he is the author of more than fifteen books and the president of The Malphurs Group (www.malphursgroup .com), a training and consulting organization.

Steve Stroope (MDiv, Southwestern Seminary) is senior pastor of Lake Pointe Church in Rockwall, Texas. He provides ministry coaching to partnership churches and pioneer missionaries worldwide and provides individual and church consulting on a limited basis. (For more information, contact strategic@lakepointe.org.)

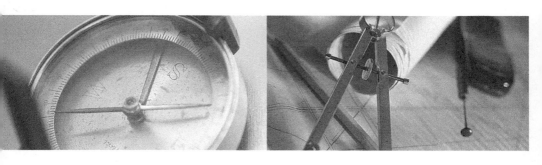

DATE DUE

Demco, Inc. 38-293